KT-571-183

GoodFood magazine

101 ONE-POT DISHES

If you have a passion for food, cooking and entertaining then
try *BBC Good Food Magazine*. Each issue is packed with delicious
up-to-the-minute recipes based on seasonal ingredients, bringing
you a tantalizing feast of food and drink! Call us on 0870 444 7017
and SAVE 25% on the cover price (please quote ref. BOOK06).
Offer valid for UK delivery only.

Published by BBC Books
BBC Worldwide Limited
80 Wood Lane
London W12 0TT

First published 2006
Reprinted 2006 (four times)
Copyright © BBC Worldwide 2006
All photographs © *BBC Good Food Magazine* 2006

All the recipes contained in this book first appeared in *BBC Good Food Magazine*.

All rights reserved. No part of this book may be reproduced in any form or by any means without permission in writing from the publisher, except by a reviewer who may quote brief passages in a review.

ISBN-13: 978 0 563 52291 1
ISBN-10: 0 563 52291 7

Commissioning Editor: Vivien Bowler
Project Editor: Sarah Reece
Designer: Kathryn Gammon
Production Controller: Peter Hunt

Set in Bookman Old Style and Helvetica
Printed and bound in Italy by LEGO SpA
Colour origination by Dot Gradations Ltd, UK

GoodFood magazine

101 ONE-POT DISHES
TRIED-AND-TESTED RECIPES

Editor
Jeni Wright

Contents

Introduction   6

Introduction

What could be simpler than cooking everything in just one pot?

At *BBC Good Food Magazine* we think it's the best kind of cooking we know. Not only does it save time and washing up, it also does away with all that juggling that comes with using different pots and pans at the same time. But perhaps most important of all, it produces the kind of meals we love to eat – food you can serve straight from stove to table for everyone to help themselves.

Most of the recipes in this book are complete meals in themselves, like the *Broccoli Lemon Chicken* pictured opposite (see page 52 for the recipe), so all they need to go with them is a quick-fix salad or some bread. Next time you're in the supermarket, take a look at the wide range of ready-cooked rice and noodles on offer – heating through is all they need.

As always at *BBC Good Food Magazine* we've done the hard work for you – we've double tested each recipe so they'll work every time, and we've included nutritional breakdowns so you know exactly what you're eating. Last but not least, we've included a special chapter of our favourite puddings and desserts that we know you will love – and they're all one-pot too. How clever is that?

Jeni Wright
BBC Good Food Magazine

Conversion tables

NOTES ON THE RECIPES
- Eggs are medium in the UK and Australia (large in America) unless stated otherwise.
- Wash all fresh produce before preparation.

OVEN TEMPERATURES

Gas	°C	Fan °C	°F	Oven temp.
¼	110	90	225	Very cool
½	120	100	250	Very cool
1	140	120	275	Cool or slow
2	150	130	300	Cool or slow
3	160	140	325	Warm
4	180	160	350	Moderate
5	190	170	375	Moderately hot
6	200	180	400	Fairly hot
7	220	200	425	Hot
8	230	210	450	Very hot
9	240	220	475	Very hot

APPROXIMATE WEIGHT CONVERSIONS
- All the recipes in this book list both imperial and metric measurements. Conversions are approximate and have been rounded up or down. Follow one set of measurements only; do not mix the two.
- Cup measurements, which are used by cooks in Australia and America, have not been listed here as they vary from ingredient to ingredient. Please use kitchen scales to measure dry/solid ingredients.

SPOON MEASURES

- Spoon measurements are level unless otherwise specified.
- 1 teaspoon = 5ml
- 1 tablespoon = 15ml
- 1 Australian tablespoon = 20ml (cooks in Australia should measure 3 teaspoons where 1 tablespoon is specified in a recipe)

APPROXIMATE LIQUID CONVERSIONS

metric	imperial	AUS	US
50ml	2fl oz	¼ cup	¼ cup
125ml	4fl oz	½ cup	½ cup
175ml	6fl oz	¾ cup	¾ cup
225ml	8fl oz	1 cup	1 cup
300ml	10fl oz/½ pint	½ pint	1¼ cups
450ml	16fl oz	2 cups	2 cups/1 pint
600ml	20fl oz/1 pint	1 pint	2½ cups
1 litre	35fl oz/1¾ pints	1¾ pints	1 quart

This hearty winter supper is a great way of getting your daily vitamins.

Chunky Winter Broth

2 × 400g cans chopped tomatoes
2 litres/3½ pints vegetable stock
4 carrots, sliced
2 × 400g cans mixed pulses,
drained and rinsed
175g/6oz spinach leaves
1 tbsp roasted red pepper pesto
crusty bread, to serve

Takes 15–20 minutes • Serves 4

1 Tip the tomatoes into a large saucepan along with the stock. Bring to the boil, turn down the heat and throw in the carrots. Gently simmer the soup until the carrots are cooked, about 15 minutes.
2 Add the pulses and spinach and heat for a few minutes, stirring, until the spinach has wilted. Spoon in the pesto and gently mix into the soup. Serve with some crusty bread.

• Per serving 219 kcalories, protein 16g, carbohydrate 34g, fat 3g, saturated fat 3g, fibre 12g, added sugar none, salt 3.16g

This is a great warming lunch or starter.
If you don't like goat's cheese, try brie instead.

Broccoli Soup with Goat's Cheese

50g/2oz butter
1 large onion, finely chopped
900g/2lb broccoli, chopped (keep florets and stalks separate)
generous grating of fresh nutmeg or ¼ tsp ground nutmeg
1 litre/1¾ pints vegetable or chicken stock
600ml/1 pint full-fat milk
100g/4oz medium-soft goat's cheese, chopped (rind and all)
croûtons, to serve (optional)

Takes 40–50 minutes • Serves 4

1 Melt the butter in a large saucepan, add the onion, broccoli stalks and nutmeg and fry for 5 minutes until soft. Add the broccoli florets and stock, then the milk. Cover and simmer gently for 8 minutes until the broccoli is tender.

2 Take out about 4 ladlefuls of broccoli, then purée the rest in the pan with a hand blender until smooth. Return the reserved broccoli to the soup and check for seasoning. (The soup will keep in the fridge for 2 days or you can cool it and freeze it for up to 2 months.)

3 To serve, reheat if necessary and scatter with the goat's cheese – and croûtons if you like.

• Per serving 371 kcalories, protein 22g, carbohydrate 16g, fat 25g, saturated fat 14.5g, fibre 6.6g, added sugar none, salt 1.67g

For an Indian version of this spicy soup, use some cooked chicken and a teaspoon of curry paste instead of the chorizo.

Chorizo and Chickpea Soup

400g can chopped tomatoes
110g pack chorizo sausage (unsliced)
140g/5oz wedge Savoy cabbage
sprinkling of dried chilli flakes
410g can chickpeas, drained and rinsed
1 chicken or vegetable stock cube
crusty bread or garlic bread, to serve

Takes 10 minutes • Serves 2

1 Put a medium pan on the heat and tip in the tomatoes followed by a canful of water. While the tomatoes are heating, quickly chop the chorizo into chunky pieces (removing any skin) and shred the cabbage.
2 Pile the chorizo and cabbage into the pan with the chilli flakes and chickpeas, then crumble in the stock cube. Stir well, cover and leave to bubble over a high heat for 6 minutes or until the cabbage is just tender. Ladle into bowls and eat with crusty or garlic bread.

• Per serving 366 kcalories, protein 23g, carbohydrate 30g, fat 18g, saturated fat 5g, fibre 9g, added sugar 0.3g, salt 4.26g

To give this simple, healthy soup a kick,
add a dash of Tabasco sauce.

Smoked Haddock Chowder

1 onion, chopped
2 potatoes, scrubbed and sliced
500ml/18fl oz vegetable stock
2 smoked haddock fillets, about
100g/4oz each, cut into chunks
418g can creamed corn
milk, to taste
handful of parsley, chopped
(optional)

Takes 20–25 minutes • Serves 2

1 Put the onion and potatoes into a large sauté pan. Pour over the vegetable stock and simmer for 6–8 minutes until the potatoes are soft, but still have a slight bite. Add the chunks of smoked haddock. Tip in the creamed corn and add a little milk if you like a thick chowder, more if you like it thinner.
2 Gently simmer for 5–7 minutes until the haddock is cooked (it should flake when prodded with a fork). Sprinkle over the parsley, if using, and ladle the chowder into bowls.

• Per serving 555 kcalories, protein 37g, carbohydrate 84g, fat 10g, saturated fat 3g, fibre 7g, added sugar none, salt 0.3g

A great soup for freezing ahead. Just reheat, make cheese on toast if you like – it's very tasty with edam – and serve.

Autumn Vegetable Soup

1 leek, chopped quite small
2 carrots, chopped quite small
1 potato, peeled and chopped quite small
1 garlic clove, finely chopped
1 tbsp finely chopped fresh rosemary
425ml/¾ pint vegetable stock
½ tsp sugar
2 × 400g cans chopped tomatoes
410g can chickpeas, drained and rinsed
3 tbsp chopped fresh parsley
cheese on toast or buttered toast, to serve (optional)

Takes 30–40 minutes • Serves 4

1 Put the vegetables into a large saucepan with the garlic, rosemary, stock and sugar. Season and stir well, then bring to a simmer. Cover and cook gently for 15 minutes or until the vegetables are just tender.
2 Whizz the tomatoes in a food processor or blender until smooth, then tip into the vegetables with the chickpeas and parsley. Gently heat through, stirring now and then. Taste for seasoning and serve hot – with cheese on toast or buttered toast if you like.

• Per serving 151 kcalories, protein 9g, carbohydrate 25g, fat 2g, saturated fat none, fibre 6.9g, added sugar 0.7g, salt 1.14g

For an even more authentic meal, serve this rich and creamy soup with some ready-cooked Thai fragrant rice.

Thai Chicken and Coconut Soup

2 × 400g cans coconut milk
3 tbsp fish sauce
4cm/1½in piece fresh root ginger or galangal, peeled and finely chopped
2 lemongrass stalks, finely sliced
6 kaffir lime leaves or strips of lime zest
1 fresh red chilli, chopped
2 tsp light muscovado sugar
500g/1lb 2oz boneless, skinless chicken breasts, cut into small bite-sized pieces
2 tbsp lime juice
good handful of fresh basil and coriander, roughly chopped

Takes 35–40 minutes • Serves 4

1 Tip all the ingredients except the chicken, lime juice and herbs into a large saucepan, bring to a gentle simmer and cook uncovered in a relaxed bubble for 5 minutes.
2 Add the chicken, cover and simmer for 8–10 minutes or until tender. Stir in the lime juice, then scatter over the herbs before serving.

• Per serving 479 kcalories, protein 35g, carbohydrate 10g, fat 34g, saturated fat 28.3g, fibre none, added sugar 2.8g, salt 2.96g

Nothing compares with freshly made tomato soup. Wait until the autumn when tomatoes are at their tastiest.

Provençal Tomato Soup

2 tbsp olive oil
1 onion, finely chopped
1 carrot, finely chopped
1 celery stick, finely chopped
2 tsp tomato purée, or to taste
1kg/2lb 4oz ripe tomatoes,
quartered
2 bay leaves
good pinch of sugar, or to taste
1.2 litres/2 pints vegetable stock

TO SERVE (OPTIONAL)
4 tbsp crème fraîche
small handful of basil leaves

Takes 1½–1¾ hours • Serves 4

1 Heat the oil in a large saucepan and gently fry the onion, carrot and celery for 10 minutes until softened and lightly coloured. Stir in the tomato purée. Tip in the tomatoes and add the bay leaves and sugar. Season to taste. Stir well, cover and cook gently for 10 minutes until the tomatoes reduce down slightly.
2 Pour in the stock, stir and bring to the boil. Cover and cook gently for 30 minutes, stirring once or twice. Remove the bay leaves. Purée the soup in the pan with a hand blender until fairly smooth, then pour through a sieve to remove the tomato skins and seeds.
3 Return the soup to the pan and reheat. Taste and add more sugar, and salt and pepper if you like, plus some more tomato purée for a deeper colour. Serve hot, topped with crème fraîche and basil leaves, if you like.

• Per serving 124 kcalories, protein 4g, carbohydrate 13g, fat 7g, saturated fat 0.9g, fibre 3.7g, added sugar 0.5g, salt 1.09g

The just-wilted watercress and mint add a fresh and peppery flavour to this speedy, tasty soup.

Three Green Vegetable Soup

knob of butter or splash of olive oil
bunch of spring onions, chopped
3 courgettes, chopped
200g/8oz podded fresh or frozen peas
850ml/1½ pints vegetable stock
85g bag trimmed watercress
large handful of mint
2 rounded tbsp Greek yogurt, plus extra to serve

Takes 15 minutes • Serves 4

1 Heat the butter or oil in a large saucepan, add the spring onions and courgettes and stir well. Cover and cook for 3 minutes, add the peas and stock and return to the boil. Cover and simmer for a further 4 minutes, then remove from the heat and stir in the watercress and mint until they are wilted.
2 Purée in the pan with a hand blender, adding the yogurt halfway through. Add seasoning to taste. Serve hot or cold, drizzled with extra yogurt.

• Per serving 100 kcalories, protein 8g, carbohydrate 9g, fat 4g, saturated fat 2g, fibre 4g, added sugar none, salt 0.81g

For a prepare-ahead dinner-party starter, freeze the soup
at the end of stage 2 and reheat just before serving.

Cannellini Bean Soup

1 tbsp olive oil
4 shallots, finely chopped
2 garlic cloves, finely chopped
1 carrot, finely chopped
2 celery sticks, finely chopped
2 leeks, finely chopped
140g/5oz streaky bacon, finely chopped
1.4 litres/2½ pints chicken or vegetable stock
2 bay leaves
2 tsp chopped fresh oregano or marjoram or ½ tsp dried
2 × 425g cans cannellini beans, drained and rinsed

TO SERVE
handful of flatleaf parley, chopped
extra virgin olive oil
6 tiny parsley sprigs

Takes about 1 hour • Serves 6

1 Heat the oil in a large saucepan and tip in the shallots, garlic, carrot, celery, leeks and bacon. Cook over a medium heat for 5–7 minutes, stirring occasionally, until softened but not browned.
2 Pour in the stock, then add the bay leaves and oregano or marjoram. Season and bring to the boil, cover the pan and simmer gently for 15 minutes. Tip in the beans, cover again and simmer for a further 5 minutes.
3 To serve, taste for seasoning and swirl in the chopped parsley. Ladle into warm bowls and top each with a drizzle of olive oil and a parsley sprig.

• Per serving 214 kcalories, protein 13g, carbohydrate 19g, fat 10g, saturated fat 3g, fibre 6g, added sugar none, salt 1.78g

No chopping must make this the easiest soup in the book! Try blitzing the soup with a handful of mint leaves for an extra-fresh flavour.

Chilled Pea and Watercress Soup

454g pack frozen peas
85g bag trimmed watercress, roughly torn
850ml/1½ pints vegetable stock
grated zest and juice of 1 small lemon
4 tbsp natural yogurt
ice cubes, to serve

Takes 10–15 minutes • Serves 4

1 Put all the ingredients, except the yogurt and ice, in a blender. Don't overfill your machine – you may need to do this in two batches. Whizz everything for a couple of minutes until smooth and speckled with the watercress.

2 Season if you want to, then serve straight away or chill until needed. The soup will keep in an airtight container in the fridge for up to 2 days (give it a stir before serving) or can be frozen for up to 1 month.

3 Serve drizzled with yogurt and drop in an ice cube or two to make it even more refreshing.

• Per serving 86 kcalories, protein 8g, carbohydrate 11g, fat 1g, saturated fat 1g, fibre 6g, added sugar none, salt 0.73g

A brilliant way of using up Christmas leftovers. And the spicy flavours make a welcome change.

Perky Turkey Soup

1 tbsp olive oil
1 large onion, halved and sliced into thin strips
1 red pepper, seeded and sliced into thin strips
2 tsp ground coriander
¼–½ tsp chilli flakes
3 tbsp basmati or long-grain rice
1.5 litres/2¾ pints turkey or chicken stock
250g/9oz cooked turkey meat, cut into thin strips
410g can chickpeas, drained and rinsed
handful of fresh coriander or flatleaf parsley, roughly chopped

Takes 25–35 minutes • Serves 4

1 Heat the oil in a large saucepan, add the onion and fry for 5 minutes or so, stirring every now and then until it starts to soften.
2 Add the red pepper, ground coriander, chilli and rice and stir for about 1 minute. Pour in the hot stock, stir in the turkey and chickpeas and season well. Bring to the boil, cover and simmer for 8–10 minutes, until the vegetables and rice are tender. Stir in the fresh coriander or parsley and serve.

• Per serving 291 kcalories, protein 27g, carbohydrate 27g, fat 9g, saturated fat 2g, fibre 4g, added sugar none, salt 1.78g

An unusual and tasty dish for vegetarians. For meat-lovers,
fry 4 sliced chorizo sausages along with the onions and celery.

Moroccan Chickpea Soup

1 tbsp olive oil
1 medium onion, chopped
2 celery sticks, chopped
2 tsp ground cumin
600ml/1 pint vegetable stock
400g can chopped tomatoes with garlic
400g can chickpeas, drained and rinsed
100g/4oz frozen broad beans
grated zest and juice of ½ lemon
large handful of coriander or parsley, and flatbread, to serve

Takes 20–25 minutes • Serves 4

1 Heat the oil in a large saucepan, then fry the onion and celery gently for 10 minutes until softened, stirring frequently. Tip in the cumin and fry for another minute.
2 Turn up the heat, then add the stock, tomatoes and chickpeas, plus a good grind of black pepper. Simmer for 8 minutes. Throw in the broad beans and lemon juice and cook for a further 2 minutes.
3 Season to taste, then top with a sprinkling of lemon zest and chopped herbs. Serve with flatbread.

• Per serving 148 kcalories, protein 9g, carbohydrate 17g, fat 5g, saturated fat 1g, fibre 6g, added sugar none, salt 1.07g

The perfect soup to start a Sunday lunch in winter.
The chilli oil is the perfect foil to the mealiness of the beans.

White Bean Soup with Chilli Oil

500g/1lb 2oz dried butter beans, soaked overnight
2 tbsp vegetable oil
1 medium onion, chopped
1 garlic clove, chopped
2 carrots, chopped
2 celery sticks, chopped
1.4 litres/2½ pints vegetable stock
2 bay leaves
2–3 fresh thyme sprigs, plus extra for sprinkling
chilli oil, for drizzling

Takes 1½–1¾ hours, plus overnight soaking • Serves 6

1 Drain the beans. Shuck off and discard the skins by pinching the beans between finger and thumb. Put the beans in a colander, rinse and drain.

2 Heat the oil in a pan and fry the onion and garlic for 1–2 minutes. Tip in the carrots and celery and fry gently for 2–3 minutes. Add the beans, stock, bay and thyme with some pepper, and bring to the boil. Reduce the heat, cover and simmer for 20–25 minutes, skimming off any scum, until the beans are soft.

3 Cool the soup for 10 minutes, discard the bay and thyme, then purée in the pan with a hand blender until quite smooth. Check for seasoning and reheat if necessary, then serve with a drizzle of chilli oil and a sprinkling of thyme leaves.

• Per serving 319 kcalories, protein 18g, carbohydrate 49g, fat 7g, saturated fat 1g, fibre 15g, added sugar none, salt 0.89g

Pesto and parmesan add flavour to this simple and healthy soup.
Stir in the zest of a lemon at the end for even more of a zing.

Summery Soup with Pesto

1 courgette, halved and very thinly sliced
200g/8oz frozen peas
250g bag ready-cooked basmati rice
100g bag baby spinach
600ml/1 pint vegetable or chicken stock
4 tbsp pesto
olive oil, for drizzling (optional)
grated parmesan, for sprinkling
crusty bread, to serve

Takes 15–20 minutes • Serves 4

1 Tip the courgette and peas into a large bowl and cover with boiling water. Cover the bowl, then leave for 3 minutes until the vegetables have softened slightly.
2 Drain the vegetables, then put back into the bowl along with the rice and spinach leaves. Pour over the hot stock, then cover and leave for another 2 minutes until the rice is heated through and the spinach has wilted.
3 Season to taste, then ladle the soup into serving bowls. Add a swirl of pesto, olive oil, if using, and the grated parmesan. Serve with crusty bread.

• Per serving 176 kcalories, protein 9g, carbohydrate 25g, fat 5g, saturated fat 2g, fibre 4g, added sugar none, salt 1.4g

A simple method and lovely Mediterranean flavours and colours make this a versatile dish, perfect for either a family supper or a dinner party.

Roasted Ratatouille Chicken

1 onion, cut into wedges
2 red peppers, seeded and cut into chunks
1 courgette (about 200g/8oz), cut into chunks
1 small aubergine (about 300g/10oz), cut into chunks
4 tomatoes, halved
4 tbsp olive oil, plus extra for drizzling
4 chicken breasts, skin on (about 140g/5oz each)
a few rosemary sprigs (optional)

Takes 50–60 minutes • Serves 4

1 Preheat the oven to 200°C/Gas 6/fan oven 180°C. Lay all the vegetables and the tomatoes in a shallow roasting tin. Make sure they have lots of room – overcrowding will slow down the cooking. Pour over the olive oil and give the vegetables a good mix round until they are well coated (hands are easiest for this).

2 Nestle the chicken breasts on top of the vegetables and tuck in some rosemary sprigs if you have them. Season everything with salt and black pepper and drizzle a little oil over the chicken. Now roast for about 35 minutes until the vegetables are soft and the chicken is golden. Drizzle with oil before serving.

• Per serving 318 kcalories, protein 37g, carbohydrate 13g, fat 14g, saturated fat 2g, fibre 4g, added sugar none, salt 0.25g

Low-fat, delicious and healthy –
and all in one pot, too!

Quick Meatball Casserole

500g/1lb 2oz turkey mince
small bunch of parsley, chopped
1 tbsp olive oil
2 large onions, chopped
2 garlic cloves, crushed
450g/1lb carrots, quartered, then cut into chunks
450g/1lb potatoes, peeled and cut into chunks
1 tbsp paprika
500g jar passata (sieved tomatoes)

Takes 45–50 minutes • Serves 4

1 Mix the turkey mince with half the chopped parsley, and salt and pepper to taste, then shape into 12 balls. Heat the oil in a large non-stick pan or flameproof casserole and fry the meatballs for 4–5 minutes, shaking the pan occasionally, until the meat is browned all over.

2 Add the chopped onions, garlic, carrots, potatoes and 300ml/½ pint water to the pan. Bring to the boil, cover and simmer for 15 minutes.

3 Stir in the paprika, passata and half the remaining parsley. Bring to the boil, cover and cook for a further 10–15 minutes or until the potatoes and carrots are tender. Season to taste and sprinkle with the remaining parsley to serve.

• Per serving 330 kcalories, protein 32g, carbohydrate 38g, fat 6g, saturated fat 1.5g, fibre 6g, added sugar none, salt 0.38g

This amazingly quick and tasty dish works well with fresh salmon, too. Just cook for 3 minutes on each side and leave out the bacon.

Chicken with Creamy Bacon Penne

1 tbsp olive oil
2 boneless, skinless chicken breasts
100g/4oz smoked lardons
(chopped bacon)
4 tbsp dry white wine
100g/4oz frozen petits pois
5 tbsp double cream
220g pack 'instant' cooked penne

Takes 10 minutes • Serves 2

1 Heat the oil in a deep non-stick frying pan, add the chicken breasts and scatter with the lardons. Leave to cook over a high heat for 4 minutes while you gather the other ingredients together.
2 Turn the chicken over in the pan, give the lardons a stir, then pour in the wine and let it bubble over a high heat until it has virtually evaporated. Now add the peas, cream and penne, season and stir well. Cover the pan and cook for 4 minutes more until the chicken is cooked all the way through. Serve straight away.

• Per serving 639 kcalories, protein 48g, carbohydrate 24g, fat 38g, saturated fat 17g, fibre 3g, added sugar none, salt 1.86g

One of the joys of one-pot cooking is putting dishes into the oven well in advance and then forgetting about them until serving time.

Ham and Beans with Orange

250g/9oz dried haricot beans, soaked overnight
2 oranges
2 tbsp olive oil
1 large onion, chopped
2 celery sticks, chopped
450g/1lb piece gammon, cut into large chunks
1 tbsp paprika
3 tbsp dark muscovado sugar
1 tbsp black treacle or molasses
2 tbsp white wine vinegar
2–3 tbsp tomato purée
4 whole cloves

Takes 2½ hours, plus overnight soaking • Serves 4

1 Drain and rinse the beans, then tip them into a pan and pour in 1.4 litres/2½ pints boiling water. Bring to the boil, cover and simmer for 30 minutes.

2 Meanwhile, preheat the oven to 180°C/Gas 4/fan oven 160°C. Grate the zest from the oranges; set aside. Heat the oil in a large flameproof casserole. Add the onion and celery and fry, stirring occasionally, for 8 minutes, until the onion is golden. Add the ham and paprika and stir for 1 minute, then tip in the orange zest, sugar, treacle, vinegar, tomato purée and cloves. Stir well.

3 Tip the beans and cooking liquid into the casserole, cover and cook for 1 hour. Remove the lid and cook for a further hour. Peel the oranges and cut the flesh into chunks. Stir into the beans, with plenty of seasoning.

• Per serving 493 kcalories, protein 37g, carbohydrate 63g, fat 12g, saturated fat 3g, fibre 13g, added sugar 19g, salt 2.85g

You can use any leftover vegetables for
this simple weekend supper.

Sausage and Leek Hash

2 tbsp olive oil
6 plump sausages
6 potatoes, thinly sliced
350g/12oz thinly sliced leeks (or
broccoli or cabbage)
1 tbsp creamed horseradish sauce,
or more to taste
100g/4oz mature cheddar or
gruyère, grated

Takes 30–35 minutes • Serves 4

1 Heat half of the oil in a large heavy-based frying pan. Add the sausages and fry gently for 8–10 minutes until well browned. Remove the sausages, then slice them on the diagonal and set aside.
2 Turn the heat to medium and add the remaining oil. Add the potatoes and leeks and give everything a good stir. Cook until the potatoes and leeks are tender and beginning to brown, turning them over from time to time. This will take 15–20 minutes.
3 Toss the sausages back in along with the horseradish, to taste, and heat through for a further 2–3 minutes. Take the pan off the heat, sprinkle in the cheese, season well and stir gently to combine. Serve.

• Per serving 534 kcalories, protein 24g, carbohydrate 35g, fat 34g, saturated fat 13.5g, fibre 4g, added sugar 0.3g, salt 2.46g

Try taleggio, ripe brie, dolcelatte or Le Roulé
if you don't like goat's cheese.

Chicken and Thyme Bake

4 part-boned chicken breasts
140g/5oz firm goat's cheese, sliced
bunch of fresh thyme
500g pack cherry tomatoes
olive oil, for drizzling
splash of dry white wine
French bread or ready-cooked
saffron rice, to serve

Takes 35–40 minutes • Serves 4

1 Preheat the oven to 190°C/Gas 5/fan oven 170°C. Loosen the skin from the chicken breasts and stuff with the slices of goat's cheese and a sprig of thyme. Put in a shallow ovenproof dish.

2 Halve the cherry tomatoes and scatter around the chicken with a few more sprigs of thyme, a drizzle of olive oil and splash of white wine. Season with pepper, and salt if you wish.

3 Bake for 25–30 minutes until the chicken is tender and golden. Serve with crusty French bread to mop up the juices or some saffron rice.

• Per serving 330 kcalories, protein 40g, carbohydrate 5g, fat 16g, saturated fat 8g, fibre 1g, added sugar none, salt 1.24g

Palm oil is an authentic African ingredient that adds a rich red colour – look for oil from Ghana or Sierra Leone in ethnic food shops.

Lamb in Palava Sauce

1 red chilli, seeded and chopped
2.5cm/1in piece fresh root ginger, peeled and roughly chopped
2 garlic cloves, peeled
1 onion, half roughly chopped and half sliced
1 tbsp tomato purée
400g can tomatoes
6 tbsp palm or vegetable oil
500g/1lb 2oz lean lamb, cut into 2.5cm/1in cubes
300ml/½ pint lamb, chicken or vegetable stock
200g/8oz fresh spinach leaves, roughly shredded
2 eggs, beaten

Takes 1¼–1½ hours • Serves 4

1 Blitz the chilli, ginger, garlic, chopped onion, tomato purée and tomatoes in a food processor until chopped together to make a sauce.

2 Heat the oil in a large frying pan and fry the sliced onion for 2 minutes. Add the lamb and stir fry over a highish heat for 6–7 minutes until starting to brown. Pour the tomato sauce over the lamb and bubble rapidly for 2–3 minutes, then stir in the stock and add seasoning to taste. Cover and simmer gently for 40–50 minutes, stirring occasionally, until the lamb is tender and the sauce has thickened.

3 Stir the spinach into the sauce so it wilts, then simmer for 2–3 minutes. Drizzle in the egg and continue to simmer for 2 minutes until just set. Serve straight from the pan.

• Per serving 421 kcalories, protein 32g, carbohydrate 3g, fat 31g, saturated fat 9g, fibre 1.5g, added sugar none, salt 0.6g

Tender-stem broccoli is ideal for this dish as it cooks so quickly. Add a couple of minutes to the cooking time if you're using ordinary broccoli.

Broccoli Lemon Chicken

1 tbsp groundnut oil or sunflower oil
340g pack mini chicken breast fillets (sometimes called goujons)
2 garlic cloves, sliced
200g pack tender-stem broccoli, stems halved if very long
200ml/7fl oz chicken stock
1 heaped tsp cornflour
1 tbsp clear honey or 2 tsp golden caster sugar
grated zest of ½ lemon and juice of 1 lemon
large handful of roasted cashews

Takes 15–25 minutes •
Serves 2 generously

1 Heat the oil in a large frying pan or wok. Add the chicken and fry for 3–4 minutes until golden. Remove from the pan and add the garlic and broccoli. Stir fry for a minute or so, then cover and cook for 2 minutes more, until almost tender.
2 Mix the stock, cornflour and honey or sugar well, then pour into the pan and stir until thickened. Tip the chicken back into the pan and let it heat through, then add the lemon zest and juice and the cashew nuts. Stir, then serve straight away.

• Per serving 372 kcalories, protein 48g, carbohydrate 15g, fat 13g, saturated fat 2g, fibre 3g, added sugar 6g, salt 0.69g

Baked beans are great, cheap comfort food,
and they're nutritious, too.

Sunday Brunch Beans

2 tbsp vegetable oil
1 potato, thinly sliced (unpeeled)
200g can corned beef, sliced
400g can baked beans
splash of Worcestershire sauce

Takes 20–25 minutes •
Serves 2 (easily doubled)

1 Heat the oil in a frying pan until hot, add the potato slices and fry for 7–10 minutes or until golden and crisp.
2 Push the potatoes to one side, add the corned beef and fry undisturbed for a couple of minutes. Tip in the baked beans, add a splash of Worcestershire sauce and stir gently until the beans are hot.

• Per serving 510 kcalories, protein 37g, carbohydrate 40g, fat 23g, saturated fat 6.4g, fibre 8.1g, added sugar 6.9g, salt 4.93g

It's so easy to recreate this classic Indian dish that you'll never order a takeaway again.

Chicken Biryani

2 tbsp vegetable oil
6 large chicken thighs, skin on
1 large onion, finely sliced
2 tbsp curry powder (hot if you like it, mild for tamer curries)
350g/12oz easy-cook long-grain rice
700ml/1¼ pints chicken or vegetable stock
250g/9oz frozen peas

Takes 50–60 minutes • Serves 6

1 Preheat the oven to 200°C/Gas 6/fan oven 180°C. Heat the oil in a large sauté pan and fry the chicken thighs, skin side down, for 8–10 minutes until the skin is golden and crispy. Tip in the onion and continue to cook for 5 minutes until the onion softens. Sprinkle in the curry powder and cook for 1 minute more, then stir in the rice and pour over the stock. Bring the stock to the boil.
2 Cover the pan and bake for 30 minutes until all the liquid has been absorbed and the rice is cooked. Stir in the peas and leave the rice to stand for a few minutes before serving.

• Per serving 445 kcalories, protein 32g, carbohydrate 57g, fat 12g, saturated fat 3g, fibre 2g, added sugar none, salt 0.5g

A low-fat, one-pot dish that's perfect for a family supper.
Serve with ready-cooked rice, available from supermarkets.

Pork and Apple Braise

500g/1lb 2oz pork tenderloin
1 tbsp plain flour, seasoned
2 tbsp olive oil
1 onion, chopped
1 Cox's apple, cored and cut into thin wedges, skin on
300ml/½ pint chicken or vegetable stock
2 bay leaves
1 tbsp wholegrain mustard
2 tbsp chopped flatleaf parsley

Takes 40–45 minutes • Serves 4

1 Cut the pork crossways into 2cm/¾in slices and coat in the seasoned flour. Heat 1 tablespoon of the oil in a large frying pan and fry the pork in small batches, then remove and set aside.

2 Fry the onion in the remaining oil until soft and golden brown. Add the apple and fry until it has slightly caramelised. Slowly stir in the stock, scraping up any bits from the bottom of the pan.

3 Return the pork to the pan and add the bay leaves and mustard. Bring to a simmer and cook for 15–20 minutes, adding a little more water or stock if necessary. Stir in the parsley and season to taste before serving.

• Per serving 248 kcalories, protein 29g, carbohydrate 9g, fat 11g, saturated fat 2g, fibre 2g, added sugar none, salt 0.41g

Look out for jars of ready-chopped ginger and chillies, and pouches of gujarati masala, in larger supermarkets.

Curry in a Hurry

1 tbsp sunflower oil
1 red onion, thinly sliced
1 garlic clove
2 tsp ready-prepared ginger from a jar
½–1 tsp ready-chopped chillies from a jar
200g can chopped tomatoes
250g/9oz boneless, skinless chicken breasts, chopped
2tsp gujarati masala or garam masala
3 tbsp low-fat yogurt
handful of coriander leaves, roughly chopped or torn
garlic and coriander naan bread, to serve

Takes 15 minutes •
Serves 2 (easily doubled)

1 Heat the oil in a pan, add the onion and fry until coloured. Crush the garlic into the pan, add the ginger and chillies and cook briefly. Add the tomatoes and a quarter of a can of water and bring to the boil. Simmer for 2 minutes, add the chicken and masala, cover and cook for 5–6 minutes.
2 Reduce the heat to a simmer, then stir in the yogurt, a tablespoon at a time. Sprinkle with coriander and serve with warm garlic and coriander naans.

• Per serving 252 kcalories, protein 34g, carbohydrate 11g, fat 8g, saturated fat 1.3g, fibre 1.8g, added sugar none, salt 0.46g

A great dish for everyone to help themselves from. A green salad, dressed lightly with olive oil and lemon juice, is all you need to go with it.

Summer Pork and Potatoes

olive oil, for drizzling
750g/1lb 10oz new potatoes, scrubbed and sliced
500g/1lb 2oz vine-ripened tomatoes, sliced
leaves of 3–4 rosemary sprigs, finely chopped
2 garlic cloves, chopped
4 pork chops or steaks
green salad, to serve

Takes 1¼–1½ hours • Serves 4

1 Preheat the oven to 200°C/Gas 6/fan oven 180°C. Drizzle a little olive oil over the base of a shallow ovenproof dish that is wide enough to take the chops in one layer. Arrange rows of potatoes and tomatoes across the dish, seasoning with salt and pepper as you go and sprinkling with half the rosemary and all the garlic.
2 Drizzle a couple more tablespoons of olive oil over the vegetables and bake for 30 minutes, then sit the pork on top, season and sprinkle with the remaining rosemary. Return to the oven for 35–45 minutes, until the pork and potatoes are tender. Serve with a green salad.

• Per serving 527 kcalories, protein 25g, carbohydrate 35g, fat 33g, saturated fat 11g, fibre 3g, added sugar none, salt 0.2g

Try using a whole preserved lemon from a jar
instead of half a lemon.

Moroccan Lemon Chicken

1kg pack boneless, skinless chicken
thigh fillets
1 onion, chopped
3 garlic cloves, crushed
1 tbsp pilau rice seasoning
2 tbsp olive oil
½ lemon, finely chopped –
the zest, pith and flesh
100g pack whole blanched almonds
140g/5oz green olives (the ones with
stones in taste best)
250ml/9fl oz chicken stock
large handful of coriander or flatleaf
parsley, chopped

Takes 40–45 minutes • Serves 4

1 Toss the chicken with the onion, garlic,
rice seasoning and oil in a microwave dish.
Microwave on High for 8 minutes until
everything is beginning to sizzle and the
chicken is starting to change colour.
2 Toss the lemon, almonds and olives over
the chicken. Pour in the stock and stir,
keeping the chicken in a single layer.
3 Cover the dish with cling film, pierce a
few times to allow the steam to escape,
then return to the microwave for another
20 minutes until the liquid is bubbling
vigorously and the chicken is cooked.
Leave to stand for a few minutes before
stirring in the coriander or parsley, then serve.

• Per serving 488 kcalories, protein 49g, carbohydrate
8g, fat 29g, saturated fat 5g, fibre 3g, added sugar
none, salt 2.68g

Ready-sliced, cooked, long-life potatoes make this
a really speedy supper dish.

Frying-pan Sausage Hotpot

1 tbsp vegetable oil
6 plump good-quality sausages with herbs
splash of red wine (if you have some)
175ml/6fl oz vegetable stock
3 tbsp ready-prepared caramelised red onions
400g pack cooked sliced long-life potatoes

Takes 25–35 minutes • Serves 3

1 Heat the oil in a medium frying pan (one the sausages will fit in fairly snugly). Add the sausages and fry for 8–10 minutes, turning them often. Preheat the grill to high. Splash a couple of tablespoons of red wine, if you are using it, into the pan, then pour in the stock and stir in the caramelised red onions. Allow the mixture to bubble for 3–4 minutes, so it thickens a little and turns into a rich gravy. Remove from the heat.
2 Spread the potatoes so they roughly cover the sausages and gravy. Put the frying pan under the grill for about 8 minutes until the potatoes turn crisp and golden. Serve while bubbling and hot – there is no need to add seasoning.

• Per serving 578 kcalories, protein 20g, carbohydrate 36g, fat 40g, saturated fat 14g, fibre 4g, added sugar 1g, salt 5.07g

You can leave the chicken to marinate in the fridge
for up to a day, if you like.

Crispy-skin Chicken Thighs

8 plump chicken thighs, skin on
2 lemons
2 tbsp chopped fresh tarragon
2 tbsp olive oil
750g/1lb 10oz new potatoes,
scrubbed and cut into wedges
2 tsp paprika, sweet or smoked
green salad, to serve

Takes 45–55 minutes • Serves 4

1 Preheat the oven to 220°C/Gas 7/fan oven 200°C. Slash the skin of each chicken thigh three times. Finely grate the zest from 1 lemon and squeeze the juice from both. Mix in a shallow dish with the tarragon, 1 tablespoon of the oil and some salt and pepper. Add the chicken and turn to coat in the marinade.

2 Spread the potato wedges over the base of a roasting tin. Toss in the remaining oil and sprinkle with paprika. Set a rack on top and arrange the chicken pieces on the rack. Roast for 30–40 minutes until the chicken is well browned and the potatoes are tender. Serve hot with a simple green salad.

• Per serving 917 kcalories, protein 64g, carbohydrate 32g, fat 60g, saturated fat 17g, fibre 2g, added sugar none, salt 0.74g

Fantastic textures and wonderful smells make this a very popular dish. You can use chicken and chicken stock if you prefer.

Turkish Lamb Pilau

small handful of pine nuts or
flaked almonds
1 tbsp olive oil
1 large onion, halved and sliced
2 cinnamon sticks, broken in half
500g/1lb 2oz lean fillet or leg
of lamb, cubed
250g/9oz basmati rice
1 lamb or vegetable stock cube
12 ready-to-eat dried apricots
handful of fresh mint leaves,
roughly chopped

Takes 25–30 minutes • Serves 4

1 Dry fry the pine nuts or almonds in a large pan until lightly toasted, then tip onto a plate. Add the oil to the pan, then fry the onion and cinnamon together until starting to turn golden. Turn up the heat, stir in the lamb, fry until the meat changes colour, then tip in the rice and cook for 1 minute, stirring all the time.
2 Pour in 500ml/18fl oz boiling water, crumble in the stock cube, add the apricots, then season to taste. Turn the heat down, cover and simmer for 12 minutes until the rice is tender and the stock has been absorbed. Toss in the pine nuts and mint and serve.

• Per serving 584 kcalories, protein 32g, carbohydrate 65g, fat 24g, saturated fat 9g, fibre 3g, added sugar none, salt 1.4g

Use a proper stir-fry oil if you can as it's infused with ginger, garlic and spices, giving a real flavour hit.

Spiced Pork with Stir-fried Greens

1 tbsp stir-fry oil or vegetable oil
250g/9oz pork escalopes, sliced into thin strips
bunch of spring onions, trimmed and sliced
175g/6oz broccoli, broken into small bite-sized florets
3 celery sticks, sliced
2 heads pak or bok choi, broken into separate leaves
2 tbsp chopped fresh coriander
finely grated zest and juice of 1 lime
a few thin slices of red chilli or a dash of sweet chilli sauce

Takes 20–30 minutes •
Serves 2 (easily doubled)

1 Heat the oil in a wok or large frying pan, add the pork and stir fry briskly for 3–4 minutes. Tip in the spring onions, broccoli and celery and stir fry over a high heat for 4 more minutes.

2 Add the pak or bok choi and cook for a minute or so until the leaves have wilted. Toss in the coriander and lime zest, squeeze in a little lime juice and add the chilli slices or sauce. Season with salt and pepper and serve straight away.

• Per serving 260 kcalories, protein 34g, carbohydrate 5g, fat 12g, saturated fat 2.3g, fibre 3.7g, added sugar none, salt 0.59g

Transform your chicken breasts into something special. As a bonus, this dish is crammed with health-boosting vegetables.

Roast Chicken and Root Vegetables

1 small celeriac, peeled and cut into 2.5cm/1in chunks
400g/14oz swede, peeled and cut into 2.5cm/1in chunks
2 large sweet potatoes, scrubbed and cut into 2.5cm/1in chunks
2 medium parsnips, scrubbed and quartered lengthways
2 large garlic cloves, thinly sliced
2 tbsp olive oil
½ tsp cumin seeds
a few sage leaves
4 boneless, skinless chicken breasts, about 140g/5oz each
4 slices prosciutto

Takes 1¼–1½ hours • Serves 4

1 Preheat the oven to 200ºC/Gas 6/fan oven 180ºC. Put the celeriac, swede, sweet potato, parsnips and garlic in a large roasting pan. Sprinkle with olive oil and cumin, and season with salt and pepper. Toss the vegetables together so they are lightly coated in oil. Put in the oven towards the top and roast for 30 minutes.
2 Meanwhile, lay a couple of sage leaves on each chicken breast, then wrap each with a slice of prosciutto to enclose.
3 Take the roasting tin from the oven and turn the vegetables over. Now lay the chicken on top. Roast for 30–35 minutes more, until the vegetables are tender and the chicken is done.

• Per serving 420 kcalories, protein 43g, carbohydrate 39g, fat 12g, saturated fat 2g, fibre 12g, added sugar none, salt 1.11g

Perfect for a quick after-work meal. And it's so easy to double or treble the quantities to feed a crowd.

Bangers and Beans in a Pan

1 tbsp vegetable oil
454g pack good-quality sausages,
each sausage chopped into three
1 small onion, chopped
3 carrots, chopped into thick slices
4 celery sticks, sliced into chunks
(finely chop the leaves
if there are any)
2 × 410g cans mixed pulses (or other
beans), drained and rinsed
400ml/14fl oz chicken or
vegetable stock
1–2 tbsp Dijon mustard (or 2 tsp
ready-made English mustard)
small handful of parsley, chopped
crusty bread, to serve

Takes 35–45 minutes • Serves 4

1 Heat the oil over a highish heat in a wide shallow pan that has a lid. Put the chopped sausages into the pan and sizzle for 5 minutes, stirring occasionally, until they are browned on all sides.
2 Throw in the onion, carrots and celery (not the leaves) and cook for 5 minutes until the onion looks see-through. Tip in the beans, give a good stir, then pour in the stock and bring to the boil, stirring. Cover and simmer for 10–15 minutes until the carrots are tender.
3 Stir in the mustard and parsley with any chopped celery leaves, then season to taste with salt and pepper. Serve hot, with chunks of crusty bread to mop up the sauce.

• Per serving 479 kcalories, protein 26g, carbohydrate 38g, fat 26g, saturated fat 8g, fibre 10g, added sugar none, salt 3.7g

A fresh and delicious dish
that's good enough to eat every day.

Chicken and Spring Vegetable Stew

2 chicken breasts, skin on
1 tbsp olive oil
200g/8oz baby new potatoes,
scrubbed and thinly sliced
500ml/18fl oz chicken stock
200g pack mixed spring vegetables
(broccoli, peas, broad beans and
sliced courgette)
2 tbsp crème fraîche
handful of fresh tarragon leaves,
roughly chopped, or ½ tsp
of dried tarragon

Takes 25–30 minutes • Serves 2

1 Fry the chicken in the olive oil in a wide pan for 5 minutes on each side. Throw in the potatoes and stir to coat. Pour over the chicken stock, cover and simmer for 10 minutes until the potatoes are almost cooked through.
2 Remove the lid and turn the heat to high. Boil the stock down until it just coats the bottom of the pan. Scatter the vegetables into the pan, cover again and cook for about 3 minutes.
3 Stir in the crème fraîche to make a creamy sauce, season with salt and pepper to taste, then add the tarragon. Serve straight from the pan.

• Per serving 386 kcalories, protein 38g, carbohydrate 23g, fat 16g, saturated fat 6g, fibre 3g, added sugar none, salt 1.5g

Get your protein hit with
this all-in-one roast.

Cheesy Chops and Chips

1kg/2lb 4oz potatoes, peeled and
thickly sliced
1 onion, thinly sliced
splash of cider, wine, water or stock
2 tbsp olive oil
4 pork chops, about 175g/6oz each
100g/4oz cheddar cheese, grated
1 tbsp wholegrain mustard
3 tbsp milk

Takes 1–1¼ hours • Serves 4

1 Preheat the oven to 230°C/Gas 8/fan oven 210°C. Toss the potatoes, onion, liquid and oil together in a large flameproof casserole. Season if you like, then bake for 20–30 minutes until the potatoes start to brown. Lay the chops on the potatoes and cook for 10 minutes more.

2 Mix the cheese, mustard and milk together. When the chops have had 10 minutes in the oven, spread the cheese mixture over them and switch the oven over to grill. Place the pan under the grill and cook for about 5 minutes until the cheese is bubbling and the potatoes are golden and crispy. Serve straight from the pan.

• Per serving 580 kcalories, protein 42g, carbohydrate 40g, fat 32g, saturated fat 14g, fibre 5g, added sugar none, salt 1.6g

With only five ingredients
this is a great after-work meal.

Pizza Chicken Melts

2 small boneless, skinless chicken breasts
1 tbsp olive oil
50g/2oz cheddar cheese, grated
4 cherry tomatoes, quartered
2 tsp pesto sauce
green salad, to serve

Takes 10–15 minutes •
Serves 2 (easily halved or doubled)

1 Preheat the grill to high. Sandwich the chicken between cling film or 2 plastic food bags and beat firmly with a rolling pin or the bottom of a saucepan to flatten. Heat the oil in a non-stick frying pan, add the chicken and cook for 2 minutes on each side until golden.
2 While the chicken cooks, mix the cheese and tomatoes together. Take the chicken from the pan and wipe out the oil with kitchen paper. Return the chicken to the pan, spread each breast with a teaspoon of pesto, then pile the cheese and tomatoes on top.
3 Put under the hot grill for a minute or so (protect the handle with foil if you think it is likely to burn), until the cheese has melted. Serve with a green salad.

• Per serving 315 kcalories, protein 37g, carbohydrate 1g, fat 18g, saturated fat 8g, fibre none, added sugar none, salt 0.68g

Liver is perfect for a mid-week meal as it's so quick to cook. Combine it with a colourful medley of vegetables for a dish bursting with flavour.

Liver and Red Pepper Stir-fry

1½ tbsp groundnut oil
200g/8oz lamb's liver, cut into strips
1 leek, diagonally sliced
1 red pepper, seeded and cut into rough squares
1 red chilli, seeded and finely chopped
1 tsp dried oregano
1 garlic clove, crushed
100g/4oz spring greens, thinly sliced
grated zest of 1 orange and 2 tbsp juice
2 tbsp medium dry sherry

Takes 25–35 minutes • Serves 2

1 Heat 1 tablespoon of the oil in a large non-stick frying pan. Add the liver and stir fry over a moderately high heat for 3 minutes until light brown – don't cook for longer or the liver will become rubbery. Remove to a plate, leaving the juices in the pan.

2 Tip the leek, red pepper and chilli into the pan with the rest of the oil and stir fry over a high heat for 2 minutes. Add the oregano, garlic and greens and stir fry for a further 30 seconds or so, until the greens have just wilted and turned a nice bright green colour.

3 Return the liver to the pan, add the orange zest and juice, and the sherry, then season. Toss everything together on a high heat and serve immediately.

• Per serving 287 kcalories, protein 27g, carbohydrate 11g, fat 14g, saturated fat 3g, fibre 4g, added sugar none, salt 0.26g

You can ensure your family stays healthy
with this low-fat feast.

Braised Pork with Fennel

1 tbsp olive oil
500g/1lb 2oz pork tenderloin, cut into chunks
1 large onion, chopped
3 garlic cloves, crushed
2 × 400g cans chopped tomatoes
2 tbsp tomato purée
½ tsp caster sugar
200ml/7fl oz vegetable stock
1 large bulb fennel
grated zest of 1 lemon

Takes 1¼–1½ hours • Serves 4

1 Heat 1 teaspoon of the oil in a large pan. Brown the pork on all sides (you may need to do this in batches). Remove from the pan with a slotted spoon and set aside. Add the remaining oil and the onion and cook over a low heat, stirring occasionally, for 5–6 minutes until the onion is soft. Stir in the garlic, tomatoes, tomato purée, sugar, stock and pork, then season. Bring to the boil.
2 Trim the fronds from the fennel, roughly chop and set aside. Cut the bulb into thin wedges and stir into the pork. Push the fennel under the surface of the sauce, lower the heat and simmer for 35–40 minutes with the lid on, until tender. Stir in the lemon zest, garnish with the chopped fennel fronds and serve.

• Per serving 242 kcalories, protein 31g, carbohydrate 12g, fat 8g, saturated fat 2g, fibre 4g, added sugar 1g, salt 0.83g

Cook this simple storecupboard risotto in the oven while you get on with something else – the result is still wonderfully creamy.

Oven-baked Risotto

250g pack smoked bacon, chopped into small pieces
1 onion, chopped
25g/1oz butter
300g/10oz risotto rice
half a glass of white wine (optional)
150g pack cherry tomatoes, halved
700ml/1¼ pint chicken stock (from a cube is fine)
50g/2oz parmesan, grated

Takes 30–35 minutes • Serves 4

1 Heat the oven to 200°C/Gas 6/fan oven 180°C. Fry the bacon pieces in an ovenproof pan or casserole dish for 3–5 minutes until golden and crisp. Stir in the onion and butter and cook for 3–4 minutes until soft. Tip in the rice and mix well until coated. Pour over the wine, if using, and cook for 2 minutes until absorbed.
2 Add the cherry tomatoes and the hot stock, then give the rice a quick stir. Cover with a tightly fitting lid and bake for 18 minutes until just cooked.
3 Stir through most of the parmesan and serve sprinkled with the remainder.

• Per serving 517 kcalories, protein 22g, carbohydrate 63g, fat 20g, saturated fat 10g, fibre 2g, added sugar none, salt 3.38g

One-pot dishes are often healthy as well as simple. This easy fish recipe proves that reducing fat doesn't mean reducing flavour.

Haddock in Tomato Basil Sauce

1 tbsp olive oil
1 onion, thinly sliced
1 small aubergine, about 250g/9oz, roughly chopped
½ tsp paprika
2 garlic cloves, crushed
400g can chopped tomatoes
1 tsp dark or light muscovado sugar
8 large basil leaves, plus a few extra for sprinkling
4 × 175g/6oz firm skinless white fish fillets, such as haddock
salad and crusty bread, to serve

Takes 40–50 minutes • Serves 4

1 Heat the oil in a large non-stick frying pan and stir fry the onion and aubergine for about 4 minutes until they start to turn golden. Cover with a lid and let the vegetables steam fry in their own juices for 6 minutes – this helps them to soften without needing any extra oil.

2 Stir in the paprika, garlic, tomatoes and sugar with ½ teaspoon salt and cook for 8–10 minutes, stirring often, until the vegetables are tender.

3 Scatter in the basil leaves, then nestle the fish in the sauce. Cover and cook for 6–8 minutes until the fish flakes easily when tested with a fork. Tear over the rest of the basil and serve with a salad and crusty bread.

• Per serving 212 kcalories, protein 36g, carbohydrate 8g, fat 4g, saturated fat 1g, fibre 3g, added sugar 1g, salt 0.5g

Accurate microwave timings ensure that everything
is cooked together perfectly.

Fish O'Leekie

1 leek, finely sliced
100g/4oz smoked lean back bacon,
chopped
500ml/18fl oz vegetable stock
300g/10oz American easy-cook rice
500g/1lb 2oz cod or haddock fillet,
skinned and cut into large chunks
3 tbsp chopped fresh parsley
grated zest and juice of 1 lemon

Takes 20–30 minutes • Serves 4

1 Put the leek and bacon in a medium microwave dish with 4 tablespoons of the stock. Cover the dish with cling film, pierce the film with a knife and microwave on High for 5 minutes.
2 Uncover the dish and stir the rice and remaining stock into the leek and bacon. Microwave on High for a further 5 minutes.
3 Gently stir in the fish chunks, cover the dish with cling film again, pierce the film with a knife and cook for a further 10 minutes until the fish and rice are done.
4 Stir in the parsley and lemon zest and juice. Leave to stand for 2–3 minutes before serving.

• Per serving 437 kcalories, protein 35g, carbohydrate 66g, fat 6g, saturated fat 1g, fibre 1g, added sugar none, salt 1.8g

You can use cooked, chopped chicken
instead of the prawns, if you prefer.

Prawn Pilau

2 tbsp korma curry paste
1 small onion, finely chopped
300g/10oz basmati rice, rinsed and
drained
700ml/1¼ pints chicken stock
150g pack cooked peeled prawns,
defrosted if frozen
cupful of frozen peas
1 red chilli, sliced into rings
handful of coriander leaves,
chopped
lemon wedges, to serve

Takes 25–30 minutes • Serves 4

1 Heat a large wide pan and dry fry the
curry paste with the onion for 4–5 minutes
until the onion begins to soften. Add the rice
to the pan and stir to coat in the curry paste.
Add the stock, then bring to the boil.
2 Cover the pan and turn the heat down
to low. Leave the rice to simmer slowly for
12–15 minutes until the liquid has been
absorbed and the rice is cooked. Turn off
the heat and stir in the prawns, peas and
chilli. Cover the pan and leave to stand for
5 minutes.
3 Fluff up the rice grains with a fork and
season if you want. Scatter over the
coriander and serve with lemon wedges.

• Per serving 340 kcalories, protein 18g, carbohydrate
65g, fat 3g, saturated fat 1g, fibre 2g, added sugar
none, salt 2.38g

This is a delicious way of
jazzing up white fish.

Parmesan-crusted Fish

50g/2oz fresh breadcrumbs
grated zest and juice of 1 lemon
25g/1oz parmesan cheese, grated
2 tbsp chopped fresh parsley
4 thick, firm, skinless white fish fillets,
such as cod, haddock, hoki
or pollock
2 tbsp olive oil
50g/2oz butter

Takes 20–30 minutes • Serves 4

1 Preheat the grill to high. Mix the breadcrumbs with the lemon zest, parmesan, parsley, and salt and pepper to taste. Season the fish.
2 Heat the oil in a frying pan. Add the fish, skinned side down, and fry for 2–3 minutes until the flesh flakes easily with a fork. Turn the fish over and sprinkle with the breadcrumb mixture, then slide the pan under the hot grill and toast the breadcrumb topping for 2–3 minutes. Add the butter to the pan in pieces, pour in the lemon juice and let the butter melt around the fish.
3 Serve the fish with the lemony butter poured over.

• Per serving 334 kcalories, protein 31g, carbohydrate 10g, fat 19g, saturated fat 8.6g, fibre 0.4g, added sugar none, salt 0.78g

Angostura bitters is a concentrated flavouring for food and drink, made from a secret blend of herbs and spices.

Caribbean Fish Stew

grated zest and juice of 1 lime
2 × 175–200g/6–8oz skinless white
fish fillets, such as cod, haddock,
hoki or pollock
juice of 2 lemons
2 × 15g packs fresh thyme, leaves
stripped from the stalks
1 tbsp dark rum
3 tbsp vegetable oil
1 onion, cut into rings
handful of coriander, chopped
2 garlic cloves, chopped
1 beefsteak tomato or 3 regular
ones, sliced
2 tsp dark muscovado sugar
dash of Angostura bitters (optional)
2 lime halves, to serve

Takes 30–40 minutes, plus optional
marinating • Serves 2

1 Spread the lime zest and juice over the base of a shallow glass or ceramic dish. Lay the fish in the dish and pour over the lemon juice. Using a mortar and pestle, crush the thyme leaves to a rough paste with ¼ teaspoon white pepper and a pinch of salt. Rub the paste all over the fish, then sprinkle over the rum. Cover and marinate at room temperature for 1 hour, if you have time.
2 Heat the oil in a deep frying pan and fry the onion for 4–5 minutes until softened. Stir in the coriander, garlic, tomato and sugar, and cook for 3–4 minutes.
3 Put the fish and its marinade in the pan, pour over 3 tablespoons water, and the bitters if you are using them. Cover and cook gently for 6–8 minutes until the fish flakes easily with a fork. Season and serve with the lime halves.

• Per serving 388 kcalories, protein 35g, carbohydrate 17g, fat 19g, saturated fat 2g, fibre 2g, added sugar 5g, salt 0.31g

A light and aromatic dish made entirely
from storecupboard ingredients.

Chilli Prawn Noodles

2 tbsp olive oil
1 onion, roughly chopped
1 heaped tbsp coriander purée (from
a tube)
pinch of dried chilli flakes,
or to taste
400g can chopped tomatoes with
garlic
1 heaped tbsp tomato purée
1 tbsp vegetable bouillon powder
150g pack straight-to-wok noodles
400g/14oz frozen prawns (large
North Atlantic ones are
tender and juicy)
sugar, optional

Takes 30–40 minutes • Serves 4

1 Heat the oil in a wok or deep frying pan.
Toss in the onion, squeeze in the coriander
purée and sprinkle over the chilli flakes to taste
(go easy at this stage). Stir fry for 5 minutes
until the onion is softened but not browned.
2 Pour in the tomatoes and 1½ canfuls hot
water, add the tomato purée and sprinkle over
the bouillon powder. Season well. Bring to a
bubble, stirring, then lower the heat and let
the sauce simmer gently for about 15 minutes
until slightly reduced but still runny.
3 When the sauce is ready, tip in the noodles
and frozen prawns. Stir well and heat through
for 2 minutes only – just to defrost the
prawns and heat through the noodles. Taste
for seasoning before serving, and add more
chilli flakes and a little sugar if you like.

• Per serving 228 kcalories, protein 22g, carbohydrate
18g, fat 8g, saturated fat 0.8g, fibre 2.1g, added sugar
none, salt 2.95g

This is a speedy supper dish that gives you a great sense of well being. Try stirring in capers, olives or peppers for a slightly different taste.

Fish with Lemon and Beans

400g can butter beans, drained and rinsed
3 tbsp lemon-infused olive oil or
3 tbsp olive oil mixed with
a little lemon juice
2 handfuls of parsley leaves, roughly chopped
100g/4oz piece chorizo sausage, skinned and chopped into small chunks
2 × 175g/6oz skinless white fish fillets, such as cod

Takes 10–15 minutes • Serves 2

1 Tip the butter beans into a shallow microwave dish. Stir in half the lemon oil, half the parsley and all the chorizo. Top with the fish fillets and the remaining oil. Cover the dish with cling film and pierce a few times. Microwave on High for 4–5 minutes, until the fish looks opaque and flakes easily.
2 Remove the fish from the dish. Stir the beans and chorizo together and spoon onto plates. Top with the fish and scatter with the remaining parsley.

• Per serving 523 kcalories, protein 48g, carbohydrate 17g, fat 30g, saturated fat 7g, fibre 6g, added sugar none, salt 2g

This is a Sweden-inspired, rich supper dish using easily available ingredients.

Smoked Salmon and Celeriac Bake

juice of 1 lemon
1 small celeriac, about 650g/1lb 7oz
2 medium baking potatoes
2 × 125g packs sliced smoked salmon
small handful of dill, chopped
1 onion, finely sliced
284ml carton double cream

Takes about 2 hours • Serves 6

1 Preheat the oven to 200°C/Gas 6/fan oven 180°C. Pour the lemon juice into a large bowl. Peel and quarter the celeriac, cut into slices the thickness of a £1 coin and toss into the lemon juice. Peel and thinly slice the potatoes and toss with the celeriac.
2 Layer the celeriac, potatoes and salmon slices in a large ovenproof dish, sprinkling dill, onion and cream over each layer, together with a little salt and plenty of black pepper. You should have 3 layers of vegetables with 2 layers of salmon, onion and dill. Finish with the remaining cream.
3 Cover the dish with foil, place on a baking tray and bake for 45 minutes. Uncover and bake for 30–40 minutes more, until the vegetables feel tender when pierced and the top is golden. Cool slightly before serving.

• Per serving 328 kcalories, protein 14g, carbohydrate 13g, fat 25g, saturated fat 15g, fibre 3g, added sugar none, salt 2.19g

Let the fresh flavours of the Mediterranean into your home
with this delicious one-pot dish.

Italian-style Roasted Fish

4 thick, firm white fish fillets, such as
cod, haddock, hoki or pollock,
skin on
1 tbsp olive oil, plus extra for
drizzling
500g/1lb 2oz cherry tomatoes,
halved
50g/2oz pitted black olives, halved
25g/1oz pine nuts
large handful of basil leaves

Takes 25–30 minutes • Serves 4

1 Preheat the oven to 200°C/Gas 6/fan oven 180°C. Season the fish. Heat the oil in a large roasting tin on top of the stove and cook the fillets, skin side down, for 2–3 minutes or until just crisp.

2 Scatter the tomatoes, olives and pine nuts around the fish, season and roast in the oven for 12–15 minutes until the fish flakes easily with a fork. Scatter with the basil leaves and drizzle with a little olive oil before serving.

• Per serving 242 kcalories, protein 30g, carbohydrate 4g, fat 12g, saturated fat 1.5g, fibre 1.7g, added sugar none, salt 0.99g

If you like spicy food, you'll love this curry, with its creamy consistency, crackling curry leaves and coconut flavour.

Kerala Prawn Curry

2 red chillies, seeded and quartered lengthways
1 small red onion, chopped
2.5cm/1in piece fresh root ginger, peeled and chopped
1 tbsp vegetable or sunflower oil
1 tsp black mustard seeds
½ tsp fenugreek seeds
14 curry leaves, fresh or dried
½ tsp turmeric
½ tsp cracked black peppercorns
150ml/¼ pint reduced-fat coconut milk
250g/9oz cooked and peeled jumbo prawns, some with their tails on

TO SERVE
squeeze of lime
chopped fresh coriander, plus a sprig or two

Takes 25–35 minutes • Serves 2

1 In a food processor, blitz the chillies, onion and ginger with 3 tablespoons water to a smoothish paste.
2 Heat the oil in a wide shallow pan or wok. Toss in the mustard and fenugreek seeds and the curry leaves – they crackle and pop – and fry for 10 seconds. Add the onion paste, lower the heat and cook without colouring for about 5 minutes. Splash in some water if it starts to catch.
3 Add the turmeric and peppercorns and stir for a few seconds. Pour in the coconut milk and bring to a simmer, stirring all the time, then lower the heat and add the prawns. Cook for 1–2 minutes until heated through. Squeeze over some lime and sprinkle with coriander before serving.

• Per serving 294 kcalories, protein 31g, carbohydrate 8g, fat 16g, saturated fat 8g, fibre none, added sugar none, salt 2.76g

Fresh mussels are surprisingly quick and easy to prepare.
Serve this dish with bread to mop up the delicious juices.

Creamy Spiced Mussels

2kg/4lb 8oz fresh mussels
150ml/¼ pint dry white wine
2 shallots, finely chopped
25g/1oz butter
1 tsp plain flour
1–2 tsp curry paste
100g/4oz crème fraîche
chopped parsley, to serve

Takes 35 minutes • Serves 4

1 Scrub the mussels in a large bowl of cold water and discard any that are open. Put in a large pan with the wine. Bring to the boil, cover and shake the pan over a high heat until the mussels are open – about 3–4 minutes.
2 Tip the mussels into a colander set over a large bowl to catch the juices. Discard any that have not opened. Strain the cooking liquid through a sieve. Keep the mussels warm.
3 Fry the shallots in the butter in the large pan until softened. Stir in the flour and curry paste and cook for 1 minute. Add the cooking liquid (except the last little bit, which may be gritty) and season with pepper, but no salt.
4 Stir in the crème fraîche and warm over a low heat until thick and glossy. Divide the mussels between four bowls and pour over the sauce. Scatter with parsley and serve.

• Per serving 285 kcalories, protein 19g, carbohydrate 6g, fat 18g, saturated fat 10g, fibre 1g, added sugar none, salt 1.27g

Risottos make the perfect microwave one-pot dish. Unlike ones cooked on the hob, you don't have to stir, leaving you free to do something else.

Easiest-ever Seafood Risotto

1 onion, finely chopped
1 bulb fennel, finely sliced
1 tbsp olive oil
300g/10oz risotto rice
500ml/18fl oz fish or vegetable stock
300g bag frozen seafood mix, defrosted
100g/4oz frozen peas
3 tbsp grated parmesan cheese
grated zest and juice of 1 lemon
handful of parsley leaves, roughly chopped

Takes 25–35 minutes • Serves 4

1 Tip the onion and fennel into a large microwave bowl, toss in the oil and microwave on High for 5 minutes. Stir in the rice, pour over the stock and cover the bowl with a plate. Microwave on High for 10–15 minutes more or until the rice is just on the verge of being cooked.

2 Stir in the seafood and peas, cover and continue to microwave on High for 2–3 minutes until the rice is cooked. Stir in the parmesan and lemon juice and leave to stand for a couple of minutes while you mix the parsley with the lemon zest. Spoon the risotto into bowls and scatter over the parsley and lemon zest. Serve.

• Per serving 419 kcalories, protein 29g, carbohydrate 64g, fat 7g, saturated fat 2g, fibre 4g, added sugar none, salt 1.16g

You can use salmon instead of cod, if you like,
in this fresh and tasty dish.

Sizzling Summer Cod

250g jar roasted mixed peppers with
herbs
250g/9oz new potatoes, scrubbed
and thickly sliced
1 red onion, cut into wedges
140g/5oz green beans, trimmed and
halved widthways
2 × 175g/6oz chunky cod fillets,
skin on
½ lemon
crusty bread, to serve

Takes 15–20 minutes • Serves 2

1 Pour all the oil from the jar of peppers into a deep frying pan. Heat the oil until bubbling, then tip in the potatoes and onion and toss in the oil. Cook for 5 minutes, stirring every now and then, until the potatoes are beginning to turn golden.

2 Carefully pour most of the oil out of the frying pan, leaving behind about 1 tablespoon. Tip in the beans and drained peppers, season and stir until well mixed. Lay the fish, skin side down, on top of the vegetables.

3 Cover the pan and cook over a medium heat for 5 minutes more or until the fish flakes easily with a fork and the vegetables are tender. Squeeze the lemon half over the fish and serve with crusty bread to mop up the juices.

• Per serving 337 kcalories, protein 37g, carbohydrate 32g, fat 8g, saturated fat 1g, fibre 5g, added sugar none, salt 0.48g

This must be the easiest fish pie ever! There are only five ingredients and three simple steps, and the finished dish is very tasty indeed.

Creamy Haddock and Tatties

400g/14oz smoked haddock
(undyed is best, but not essential),
skinned and chopped into chunks
1 trimmed leek, finely sliced
handful of parsley, chopped
142ml carton double cream
2 medium baking potatoes, about
200g/8oz each, unpeeled, sliced
as thinly as possible

Takes 15–20 minutes • Serves 2

1 Scatter the haddock, leek and parsley over the base of a shallow microwave dish and mix together with your fingers or a spoon. Drizzle over half the cream and 5 tablespoons water. Lay the potato slices over the fish and leek. Season with a little salt and plenty of black pepper, and drizzle over the remaining cream.

2 Cover the dish with cling film and pierce a few times. Microwave on High for 8–10 minutes until everything is bubbling away and the potatoes are tender when pierced with a knife. While the dish is in the microwave, preheat the grill to high.

3 Remove the cling film and put the dish under the grill until the potatoes are golden. Leave to stand for a minute or two before serving.

• Per serving 646 kcalories, protein 45g, carbohydrate 38g, fat 36g, saturated fat 22g, fibre 4g, added sugar none, salt 3.97g

Try this as a starter for
a special meal for two.

Scallops with Chilli and Lime

2 tbsp olive oil
10 scallops
2 large garlic cloves, chopped
2 tsp chopped fresh red chilli
juice of 1 lime
small handful of coriander, roughly
chopped

Takes 10–15 minutes • Serves 2

1 Heat the oil in a non-stick frying pan until hot, add the scallops and pan fry for 1 minute until golden underneath. Flip them over and sprinkle with the garlic and chilli.
2 Cook for 1 minute more, then pour over the lime juice and season with salt and pepper. Serve immediately, scattered with the coriander.

• Per serving 260 kcalories, protein 34g, carbohydrate 2g, fat 13g, saturated fat 2g, fibre 0.3g, added sugar none, salt 0.99g

Hearty and healthy, this is comfort food at its best –
ideal for a mid-week supper in the winter.

Smoked Haddock Stovies

knob of butter
splash of vegetable oil
2 onions, thinly sliced
1kg/2lb 4oz floury potatoes, such as
Maris Piper or King Edward,
peeled and thickly sliced
500g/1lb 2oz skinless smoked
haddock, cut into large chunks
handful of parsley, coarsely chopped

Takes 30–40 minutes • Serves 4

1 Heat the butter and oil in a large wide pan, add the onions and cook for 5 minutes, stirring until lightly coloured. Tip in the potatoes and cook for a further 5 minutes, stirring often, until they are also lightly coloured.
2 Pour in 425ml/¾ pint water and grind in black pepper to taste. Stir to mix, then gently stir in the fish and bring to the boil. Cover and cook for 10 minutes or until the potatoes and fish are tender. Scatter with parsley before serving.

• Per serving 307 kcalories, protein 29g, carbohydrate 39g, fat 5g, saturated fat 2g, fibre 4g, added sugar none, salt 2.5g

Even those who don't love fish will like this
simple, speedy, foolproof dish.

Cheesy Fish Grills

sunflower or olive oil, for brushing
4 chunky, skinless white fish fillets,
such as hoki or cod, about
500g/1lb 2oz total weight
4 thin, but not wafer-thin,
slices of ham
50g/2oz mature cheddar cheese,
grated
2 spring onions, sliced at an angle
green salad, to serve

Takes 15–25 minutes • Serves 4

1 Preheat the grill to high and lightly oil a
large, shallow, flameproof dish. Arrange the
fillets, skinned side down, in the dish, slightly
spaced apart, and brush with a little oil.
Grill for 2 minutes.
2 Remove the dish from the grill, turn the fish
over and top each fillet with a scrunched slice
of ham. Mix together the cheese and onions,
scatter over the fish and season with salt
and pepper. Return to the grill for 5 minutes
or until the fish flakes easily with a fork. Serve
with a green salad.

• Per serving 179 kcalories, protein 30g, carbohydrate
none, fat 6g, saturated fat 3g, fibre none, added sugar
none, salt 0.94g

An ever-popular recipe for an easy and
delicious one-pot meal.

Spicy Prawn and Chorizo Rice

2 tbsp olive oil
2 garlic cloves, finely chopped
1 large onion, finely chopped
2 red chillies, seeded and chopped
400g/14oz chorizo sausage, skinned
and cut into chunks
450g/1lb long-grain rice
1 tsp smoked paprika or 1 tbsp
ground paprika
200ml/7fl oz dry white wine
1.5 litres/2¾ pints hot chicken
stock (if using cubes, don't use
more than two)
175g/6oz frozen broad beans
or peas
400g/14oz raw shelled tiger prawns,
thawed if frozen
250g/9oz cherry tomatoes, halved
3 tbsp chopped flatleaf parsley, plus
extra for sprinkling

Takes 45–55 minutes • Serves 6

1 Heat the oil in a wide shallow pan and fry the garlic, onion, chillies and chorizo for a few minutes until the onion has softened. Stir in the rice and paprika, then add the wine and bubble away until it evaporates.
2 Pour in the stock, lower the heat and cook gently for 10 minutes, stirring occasionally. Tip in the beans or peas, season and cook for 7–10 minutes, stirring, until the rice is tender. Keep some boiling water at the ready in case you need it to keep the rice moist.
3 Stir in the prawns and tomatoes and cook for a few minutes until the prawns turn pink. Toss in the parsley and taste for seasoning before serving, sprinkled with a little more parsley.

• Per serving 624 kcalories, protein 33g, carbohydrate 75g, fat 21g, saturated fat 1g, fibre 3g, added sugar none, salt 2.15g

Serve with crusty bread to mop up
the tasty juices.

Speedy Salmon and Leeks

700g/1lb 9oz leeks, finely sliced
3 tbsp olive oil
2 tbsp wholegrain mustard
2 tbsp clear honey
juice of ½ lemon
250g pack cherry tomatoes, halved
4 × 175g/6oz skinless salmon fillets

Takes 20–25 minutes • Serves 4

1 Put the leeks into a large microwave dish and sprinkle over 2 tablespoons water. Cover the dish with cling film and pierce a couple of times with a fork. Cook on High for 3 minutes, then leave to stand for 1 minute.

2 Whisk the olive oil, mustard, honey and lemon juice together and season with a little salt and pepper. Scatter the tomatoes on top of the leeks and spoon over half the sauce.

3 Lay the salmon fillets side by side on top of the vegetables and spoon the remaining sauce over them. Replace the cling film and continue cooking on High for 9 minutes. Leave to stand for a couple of minutes before serving.

• Per serving 471 kcalories, protein 39g, carbohydrate 13g, fat 29g, saturated fat 6g, fibre 5g, added sugar 6g, salt 0.54g

For a Spanish-style version, add a pinch of saffron and a little white wine along with the tomatoes.

20-minute Seafood Pasta

1 tbsp olive oil
1 onion, chopped
1 garlic clove, chopped
1 tsp paprika
400g can chopped tomatoes
1 litre/1¾ pints chicken stock
300g/10oz spaghetti, roughly broken
240g pack mixed frozen seafood, defrosted

TO SERVE
handful of parsley leaves, chopped
4 lemon wedges

Takes 20–25 minutes • Serves 4

1 Heat the oil in a wok or large frying pan, then cook the onion and garlic over a medium heat for 5 minutes until soft. Add the paprika, tomatoes and stock, then bring to the boil.
2 Turn down the heat to a simmer, stir in the pasta and cook for 7 minutes, stirring occasionally to stop the pasta from sticking.
3 Stir in the seafood, cook for 3 minutes more until it's all heated through and the pasta is cooked, then season to taste. Sprinkle with the parsley and serve with lemon wedges.

• Per serving 370 kcalories, protein 23g, carbohydrate 62g, fat 5g, saturated fat 1g, fibre 4g, added sugar none, salt 1.4g

This is a gently spiced and very tasty curry that suits all tastes. Peas are quick-frozen within a few hours of picking, so stay deliciously fresh.

Spicy Pea Curry

2 tbsp vegetable oil
227g pack paneer (Indian cheese), torn into pieces
1 onion, thinly sliced
2 tbsp mild curry paste
450g/1lb potatoes, peeled and cut into chunks
400g can chopped tomatoes with garlic
300ml/½ pint vegetable stock
300g/10oz frozen peas
Indian bread, to serve

Takes 40–50 minutes • Serves 4

1 Heat 1 tablespoon of the oil in a large saucepan. Fry the paneer for 2–3 minutes, stirring, until crisp and golden. Remove with a slotted spoon and set aside.

2 Fry the onion in the remaining oil for 4–5 minutes until soft and just beginning to brown. Add the curry paste and fry, stirring, for 2 minutes.

3 Add the potatoes, tomatoes, stock and paneer, bring to the boil and simmer for 15 minutes. Add the peas, bring to the boil and simmer for 5 minutes longer. Season and serve with peshwari naan or other Indian bread.

• Per serving 404 kcalories, protein 20g, carbohydrate 32g, fat 22g, saturated fat 9g, fibre 7g, added sugar none, salt 2.84g

A colourful and hearty
supper dish for autumn.

Roasted Vegetables with Cheese

1 red onion
1 large butternut squash
(600–700g/1lb 5oz–1lb 9oz),
peeled, seeded and cut into large
bite-sized pieces
6 tbsp olive oil
2 tbsp chopped fresh sage leaves
1 large courgette, thickly sliced
1 tbsp balsamic or sherry vinegar
100g/4oz Lancashire cheese

Takes 40–50 minutes • Serves 2

1 Preheat the oven to 200°C/Gas 6/fan oven 180°C. Halve the onion lengthways and trim the root end, leaving a little root left on to hold the segments together. Peel each half and cut into 4 wedges. Scatter the onion and squash in a large roasting tin so they have plenty of room, and toss with 5 tablespoons of the oil, the sage and seasoning to taste. Roast for 20 minutes, stirring halfway.
2 Toss the courgette slices with the remaining oil. Remove the tin from the oven and push the squash and onion to one side. Lay the courgette slices flat on the base of the tin, season and roast for 10 minutes, until all the vegetables are tender.
3 Sprinkle the vinegar over the vegetables and toss to mix, then crumble over the cheese and toss lightly so the cheese melts a little. Serve.

• Per serving 306 kcalories, protein 8g, carbohydrate 14g, fat 25g, saturated fat 7g, fibre 3g, added sugar none, salt 0.39g

Use your own potato leftovers if you like.
Serve with a peppery rocket and watercress salad.

Potato and Mozzarella Tortilla

2 tbsp olive oil
2 × 400g packs ready-roasted potatoes (available with different flavourings from most supermarkets)
8 eggs, beaten
4 vine-ripened tomatoes, sliced
150g ball mozzarella, torn into pieces

Takes 30 minutes • Serves 6

1 Heat the oil in a large frying pan. Empty the potatoes into the pan, spread them out to cover the base, then fry for 5 minutes. Pour in the beaten eggs so they completely cover the potatoes, season well and leave the tortilla to cook on a medium heat for about 15–20 minutes, or until the base and edges have set.
2 Meanwhile preheat the grill to high. Take the tortilla off the hob and place under the grill until the top is firm, then remove from the grill and scatter over the tomatoes and mozzarella. Put the tortilla back under the grill for a further 3–5 minutes, or until the tomatoes are soft and the cheese has melted. Serve, cut into thick wedges.

• Per serving 465 kcalories, protein 28g, carbohydrate 23g, fat 32g, saturated fat 7g, fibre 3g, added sugar none, salt 0.72g

A Chinese stir-fry that's perfect for all the family. Get all the ingredients prepared first so you can toss them straight into the pan.

Quorn and Cashew Nut Stir-fry

50g/2oz cashew nuts
1 tbsp vegetable oil
200g/8oz Quorn pieces
85g/3oz small broccoli florets
85g/3oz small cauliflower florets
2 tbsp hoisin sauce
1 red or yellow pepper, seeded and sliced

Takes 15 minutes •
Serves 2 (easily doubled)

1 Tip the cashews into a wok or deep, non-stick frying pan and dry fry over a medium heat for a few minutes until toasted. Remove and set aside. Heat the oil in the wok, add the Quorn, broccoli and cauliflower and stir fry for 2 minutes.

2 Mix the hoisin sauce with 6 tablespoons boiling water, pour into the wok and add the sliced pepper. Toss for 3 minutes, or until the pepper is just tender. Add seasoning to taste and serve sprinkled with the cashews.

• Per serving 363 kcalories, protein 23g, carbohydrate 19g, fat 22g, saturated fat 2.6g, fibre 9g, added sugar 5g, salt 1.43g

Sweet red pepper sauce makes an interesting change from tomato sauces. Serve this veggie chilli with garlic bread and a salad.

Bean and Vegetable Chilli

3 tbsp olive oil
2 onions, chopped
2 tsp caster sugar
250g/9oz chestnut mushrooms, sliced
2 garlic cloves, sliced
2 tsp mild chilli powder
1 tbsp ground coriander
290–350g jar sweet red pepper sauce
300ml/½ pint vegetable stock
410g can chickpeas, drained and rinsed
410g can black-eye beans, drained and rinsed
garlic bread and mixed salad, to serve

Takes 40–50 minutes • Serves 4

1 Heat the oil in a large, heavy-based saucepan and fry the onions and sugar over a high heat until deep golden. Add the mushrooms, garlic, chilli powder and ground coriander and fry for 2–3 minutes.
2 Stir in the pepper sauce, stock, chickpeas and beans and bring to the boil. Reduce the heat, cover and simmer gently for 20 minutes. Season and serve, with garlic bread and a mixed salad.

• Per serving 303 kcalories, protein 14g, carbohydrate 36g, fat 13g, saturated fat 2g, fibre 8g, added sugar 5g, salt 1.4g

Warming and tasty, practically no preparation, superhealthy, uses storecupboard ingredients – one-pot dishes don't get better than this.

Curried Rice with Spinach

1 tbsp sunflower oil
2 garlic cloves, crushed
2 tbsp medium curry paste (Madras is a good one to use)
250g/9oz basmati rice, rinsed
450ml/16fl oz vegetable stock
400g can chickpeas, drained and rinsed
handful of raisins
175g/6oz frozen leaf spinach, thawed
handful of cashew nuts
natural yogurt, to serve (optional)

Takes 20 minutes • Serves 4

1 Heat the oil in a large, non-stick pan that has a lid, then fry the garlic and curry paste over a medium heat for 1 minute, until it smells toasty.

2 Tip the rice into the pan with the stock, chickpeas and raisins and stir well with a fork to stop the rice from clumping. Season with salt and pepper, then cover and bring to the boil. Reduce to a medium heat and cook for 12–15 minutes or until all the liquid has been absorbed and the rice is tender.

3 Squeeze the excess water from the spinach with your hands. Tip it into the pan along with 2 tablespoons hot water, then fluff up the rice with a fork, making sure the spinach is mixed in well. Toss in the cashews. Serve drizzled with natural yogurt if you like.

• Per serving 380 kcalories, protein 12g, carbohydrate 66g, fat 9g, saturated fat 1g, fibre 4g, added sugar none, salt 1.02g

The wine really adds flavour to this warming dish, and the baby vegetables look so pretty, too.

Vegetable Casserole with Dumplings

8 shallots, halved lengthways
3 tbsp light olive oil
250g/9oz new potatoes, halved
1 chilli, seeded and chopped
200g/8oz baby carrots, scraped
500g/1lb 2oz fennel, cut into wedges
300ml/½ pint fruity white wine
600ml/1 pint vegetable stock
200g/8oz green beans, halved
250g/9oz mushrooms,halved
200g/8oz baby courgettes, chopped
1 tbsp each chopped chives
and parsley

FOR THE DUMPLINGS
50g/2oz butter, cut into pieces
100g/4oz self-raising flour
50g/2oz mature cheddar cheese,
grated
3 tbsp finely chopped fresh parsley

Takes 1¾–2 hours • Serves 6

1 Fry the shallots in the oil in a flameproof casserole until softened. Add the potatoes and fry for 5–7 minutes, then add the chilli, carrots and fennel and fry until coloured. Pour in the wine and stock and bring to the boil. Season, cover and simmer for 10 minutes.
2 Make the dumplings. Rub the butter into the flour, stir in the cheese, parsley and seasoning, then stir in about 2 tablespoons water to form a soft dough. Break off small pieces and form into 20–25 dumplings.
3 Add the beans to the pan and simmer for 5 minutes, then add the mushrooms and courgettes. Bring to the boil and stir well. Place the dumplings on top. Cover and simmer for 15 minutes until the dumplings have risen. Taste for seasoning and serve sprinkled with the chives and parsley.

• Per serving 285 kcalories, protein 8g, carbohydrate 28g, fat 17g, saturated fat 7g, fibre 5.6g, added sugar none, salt 0.85g

Juicy tomatoes and creamy cheese ensure a dish with flavours that will burst in your mouth.

Greek Salad Omelette

10 eggs
handful of parsley leaves, chopped
2 tbsp olive oil
1 large red onion, cut into wedges
3 tomatoes, chopped into large chunks
large handful of black olives (pitted are easier to eat)
100g/4oz feta, crumbled

Takes 15–20 minutes • Serves 4–6

1 Preheat the grill to high. Whisk the eggs in a large bowl with the chopped parsley, pepper, and salt if you want. Heat the oil in a large, non-stick frying pan, then fry the onion wedges over a high heat for about 4 minutes until they start to brown around the edges. Add the tomatoes and olives, stir and cook for 1–2 minutes until the tomatoes begin to soften.

2 Turn the heat down to medium and pour in the eggs. Stir the eggs as they begin to set, until half cooked but still runny in places – about 2 minutes. Scatter over the feta, then slide the pan under the grill for 5–6 minutes until the omelette is puffed up and golden. Cut into wedges and serve straight from the pan.

• Per serving for four 371 kcalories, protein 24g, carbohydrate 5g, fat 28g, saturated fat 9g, fibre 1g, added sugar none, salt 2g

Use whichever vegetables are in season for this light and pretty dish. To make it richer, add 100g/4oz feta when you stir in the dill.

Spring Vegetable Pilau

1 tbsp olive oil
1 onion, chopped
300g/10oz basmati rice
700ml/1¼ pints vegetable stock
100g pack asparagus, cut into 2cm/¾in chunks
large handful of peas, fresh or frozen
large handful of broad beans, fresh or frozen
1 courgette, sliced
small bunch of dill, chopped

Takes 20 minutes • Serves 4

1 Heat the oil in a frying pan and cook the onion for 5 minutes until soft. Tip in the rice, pour over the stock and stir. Bring to the boil, then lower the heat to a simmer, cover and cook for 10 minutes or until the rice is almost tender.
2 Add the vegetables to the pan, cover and let them steam for 2 minutes. Take the pan off the heat and leave to stand, covered, for another 2 minutes to absorb any more liquid. Stir in the dill just before serving.

• Per serving 317 kcalories, protein 9g, carbohydrate 66g, fat 4g, saturated fat 1g, fibre 3g, added sugar none, salt 0.58g

Lighter than the original, this basic pasta dish is
one to experiment with.

Macaroni Cheese with Mushrooms

200g/8oz macaroni
2 leeks
6 mushrooms
4 tomatoes
2 tbsp olive oil
2 × mini Le Roulé garlic and herb
soft cheeses, or mini bries or
blue cheeses

Takes 20–25 minutes • Serves 2

1 Fill a large sauté pan with boiling water.
Tip in the macaroni and cook according to
the pack instructions until tender. (It may take
slightly longer than suggested.) Meanwhile,
trim, slice and wash the leeks, quarter the
mushrooms and roughly chop the tomatoes.
2 Drain the pasta and keep warm. Heat the
oil in the pan, add the leeks and mushrooms
and fry for 4–6 minutes until the leeks are
tender. Toss in the tomatoes at the last
minute. Season with salt if you want to, and
black pepper. Stir in the macaroni and warm
through, then crumble the cheese over and
let it melt slightly before serving.

• Per serving 619 kcalories, protein 17g, carbohydrate
85g, fat 26g, saturated fat 10g, fibre 8g, added sugar
none, salt 0.3g

Serve with warm mini naan breads. Alternatively this curry mixture makes a great low-fat filling for baked potatoes.

Mixed Vegetable Balti

1 tbsp vegetable oil
1 large onion, thickly sliced
1 large garlic clove, crushed
1 eating apple, peeled, cored and chopped into chunks
3 tbsp balti curry paste
1 medium butternut squash, peeled and cut into chunks
2 large carrots, thickly sliced
200g/8oz turnips, cut into chunks
1 cauliflower, about 500g/1lb 2oz, broken into florets
400g can chopped tomatoes
425ml/¾ pint vegetable stock
4 tbsp chopped coriander, plus extra to serve
150g carton low-fat natural yogurt

Takes 1¼–1½ hours • Serves 4

1 Heat the oil in a large pan and cook the onion, garlic and apple gently, stirring occasionally, until the onion softens – about 5–8 minutes. Stir in the curry paste.
2 Tip the fresh vegetables, tomatoes and stock into the pan. Stir in 3 tablespoons of the coriander. Bring to the boil, lower the heat, cover and cook for 30 minutes.
3 Remove the lid and cook for another 20 minutes until the vegetables are soft and the liquid has reduced a little. Season with salt and pepper.
4 Mix the remaining coriander into the yogurt to make a raita. Ladle the curry into bowls, drizzle over some raita and sprinkle with extra coriander. Serve with the remaining raita.

• Per serving 201 kcalories, protein 11g, carbohydrate 25g, fat 7g, saturated fat 1g, fibre 7g, added sugar none, salt 1.13g

Want to be practical but need some inspiration? This dish is a great way of using up potatoes and it's not as unhealthy as it looks.

Oven Egg and Chips

450g/1lb floury potatoes, such as King Edward or Maris Piper
2 garlic cloves, sliced
4 fresh rosemary sprigs or 1 tsp dried rosemary
2 tbsp olive oil
2 eggs

Takes 50–60 minutes • Serves 2

1 Preheat the oven to 220°C/Gas 7/fan oven 200°C. Without peeling, cut the potatoes into thick chips. Tip them into a roasting pan (non-stick is best) and scatter over the garlic. Strip the rosemary leaves from the sprigs and sprinkle them, or the dried rosemary, over too. Drizzle with the oil, season well, then toss the chips to coat them in oil and flavourings.

2 Oven-roast the chips for 35–40 minutes until just cooked and golden, shaking the tin halfway through.

3 Make two gaps in the chips and break an egg into each gap. Return to the oven for 3–5 minutes until the eggs are cooked to your liking.

• Per serving 348 kcalories, protein 11g, carbohydrate 40g, fat 17g, saturated fat 3g, fibre 3g, added sugar none, salt 0.22g

Paneer is a low-fat cheese often described as Indian cottage cheese, but it's firmer and keeps its shape in cooking.

Paneer in Herby Tomato Sauce

½ tsp cumin seeds
1 green chilli, seeded and chopped
4cm/1½in piece fresh root ginger, peeled and chopped
150g carton Greek yogurt
1 tsp light muscovado sugar
½ tsp garam masala
2 tbsp chopped fresh coriander leaves and stems
juice of ½ lime
3 tbsp tomato purée
250g/9oz frozen peas
227g pack paneer (Indian cheese), cut into 1cm/½in cubes
2–3 firm red tomatoes, cut into wedges
handful of roasted cashew nuts, chopped, to serve

Takes 25–35 minutes • Serves 2

1 Toast the cumin seeds in a pan to darken – about 30 seconds. Crush roughly with a rolling pin, then tip into a blender with the chilli, ginger, yogurt, sugar, garam masala, coriander, lime juice, tomato purée and 200ml/7fl oz water. Blitz until smooth.
2 Pour the sauce into the pan used to toast the cumin. Cook for 5 minutes, stirring often. Add the peas and simmer for 3–5 minutes until almost cooked.
3 Stir in the paneer and tomatoes and heat through for 2–3 minutes. Scatter with cashew nuts just before serving.

• Per serving 607 kcalories, protein 44g, carbohydrate 24g, fat 38g, saturated fat 23g, fibre 8g, added sugar 3g, salt 3.26g

Steaming is a great way of cooking food with flavourings. The results are light and tasty and retain all the freshness of the ingredients.

Summer Veggie and Tofu Bowl

1–2 carrots, cut into sticks if large
1–2 turnips, cut into wedges
1 tbsp dry sherry
2 tbsp soy sauce
1 courgette, cut into 1cm/½in slices
4–6 short asparagus spears
3 fresh shiitake or open-cup mushrooms, each sliced in four
25g/1oz butter
2 spring onions, shredded
100g/4oz smoked tofu, cubed

Takes 25 minutes • Serves 2

1 Mix the carrot and turnip with the sherry and soy sauce in a shallow heatproof bowl that will fit inside a steamer basket. Leave to marinate for 10 minutes.

2 Bring a pan of water to the boil, fit the steamer basket, then place the bowl of carrot and turnip inside. Cover and steam for 4–5 minutes.

3 Add the courgette, asparagus and mushrooms, stirring to mix. Dot with the butter, sprinkle with the spring onions, cover and continue steaming for another 3 minutes.

4 Add the tofu and continue steaming for 2 minutes. Remove the bowl and mix everything together before serving.

• Per serving 206 kcalories, protein 8g, carbohydrate 11g, fat 13g, saturated fat 6.9g, fibre 4.4g, added sugar 0.3g, salt 3.01g

This is vegetarian food at its
easiest and most comforting.

Cheesy Vegetable Hotpot

3 leeks, trimmed, roughly sliced
large knob of butter
½ small Savoy cabbage, shredded
8 chestnut mushrooms, sliced
4 tbsp crème fraîche
3 medium potatoes, peeled and
thinly sliced
1 small camembert or other rinded
soft cheese, sliced with
the rind on
1 tbsp fresh thyme leaves

Takes 35–40 minutes • Serves 4

1 In a shallow microwavable dish, toss the leeks in half the butter and microwave on High for 5 minutes until they begin to soften. Stir in the cabbage and mushrooms and add the crème fraîche. Lay the potato slices over the vegetables, pressing them down with a fish slice.

2 Dot the potatoes with the remaining butter and microwave, uncovered, for 15–20 minutes on High until they are done. Scatter over the cheese and thyme, and either microwave on High to melt for 2 minutes, or grill until crisp and brown. Leave to stand for a few minutes before serving.

• Per serving 308 kcalories, protein 15g, carbohydrate 19g, fat 20g, saturated fat 12g, fibre 5g, added sugar none, salt 0.83g

This is such a simple recipe and is welcome at any time of day – for a weekend lunch, an easy supper or even a leisurely breakfast.

Tomato Baked Eggs

900g/2lb ripe vine tomatoes
3 garlic cloves, thinly sliced
3 tbsp olive oil
4 large free-range eggs
2 tbsp chopped parsley and/or chives
toast or ciabatta, and green salad, to serve

Takes about 1 hour • Serves 4

1 Preheat the oven to 200°C/Gas 6/fan oven 180°C. Cut the tomatoes into quarters or thick wedges, depending on their size, then spread them over the base of a fairly shallow, large, ovenproof dish. Sprinkle the garlic over the tomatoes, drizzle with the oil and season well. Stir until the tomatoes are glistening, then bake for 40 minutes until softened and tinged with brown.

2 Make 4 gaps among the tomatoes, break an egg into each gap and cover the dish with foil. Return the dish to the oven for 5–10 minutes until the eggs are set to your liking. Scatter over the herbs and serve piping hot, with thick slices of toast or warm ciabatta and a green salad on the side.

• Per serving 204 kcalories, protein 9g, carbohydrate 7g, fat 16g, saturated fat 3g, fibre 3g, added sugar none, salt 0.27g

You can vary the vegetables – try sweet potatoes, sugarsnap peas and bamboo shoots – and scatter over cashew nuts.

Thai Red Squash Curry

1 small butternut squash, about 700g/1lb 9 oz
200g pack mixed mangetout and baby corn
2 tbsp sunflower oil
1–2 tbsp Thai red curry paste, to taste
400ml can coconut milk
150ml/¼ pint vegetable stock
2 tbsp soy sauce
1 tbsp light muscovado sugar
juice of ½ lime
naan bread or chapatis, to serve

Takes 30 minutes • Serves 4

1 Cut off the ends of the squash, quarter lengthways, then scoop out the fibres and seeds. Peel, then cut into chunks. Halve the baby corn lengthways.
2 Heat the oil in a saucepan and fry the paste gently for 1–2 minutes. Add the coconut milk, stock, soy sauce and sugar and bring to the boil.
3 Add the squash and baby corn, and salt to taste, cover and simmer for 10–12 minutes. Add the lime juice and mangetout, and simmer for 1 minute. Serve hot, with naan bread or chapatis.

• Per serving 283 kcalories, protein 4.4g, carbohydrate 16.2g, fat 22.6g, saturated fat 14.6g, fibre 2.2g, added sugar 5.3g, salt 1.95g

For a vegetarian crowd, swap the meat for two 400g cans of chickpeas (drained and rinsed), and increase the mushrooms to 400g/14oz.

Steak and Mushroom Goulash

750g/1lb 10oz rump or sirloin steak, trimmed and cut into thin strips against the grain
3 tbsp vegetable oil
200g/8oz chestnut mushrooms, quartered
1 tbsp paprika
900g/2lb potatoes, peeled and cut into small chunks
500g jar passata (sieved tomatoes)
about 850ml/1½ pints beef stock
150g carton natural yogurt
handful of parsley leaves, roughly chopped

Takes 50–60 minutes • Serves 8

1 Season the steak well. Heat 1 tablespoon of the oil in a large flameproof casserole over a medium-high heat. Add about a third of the steak and fry for 2–3 minutes until all the strips are browned, stirring once. Transfer the meat to a plate with a slotted spoon. Repeat with the remaining oil and meat.

2 Tip the mushrooms into the pan, lower the heat a little and fry, stirring occasionally, until they begin to colour (about 5 minutes). Sprinkle in the paprika and stir fry briefly, then tip in the potatoes and passata and enough stock to cover the potatoes. Stir well, cover and simmer for 20 minutes or until the potatoes are tender.

3 Return the meat to the pan with its juices, stir well and simmer for 5 minutes or until tender. Taste for seasoning and serve topped with the yogurt and parsley.

• Per serving 279 kcalories, protein 26g, carbohydrate 25g, fat 9g, saturated fat 2.2g, fibre 2g, added sugar 0.9g, salt 0.87g

Play around with this recipe. If you don't feel like using asparagus and broad beans, you could try broccoli sprigs and green beans instead.

Chicken with Spring Vegetables

2 tbsp olive oil
25g/1oz butter
8 large boneless, skinless chicken breasts, each cut into 3 pieces
8 shallots, halved
2 garlic cloves, roughly chopped
450g/1lb baby new potatoes, halved
450g/1lb baby carrots, scrubbed
3 tbsp plain flour
1½ tbsp Dijon mustard
425ml/¾ pint dry white wine
425ml/¾ pint chicken stock
225g/8oz asparagus tips, trimmed
225g/8oz shelled broad beans, thawed if frozen
1 tbsp lemon juice
100ml/3½fl oz double cream
handful of chopped mixed fresh parsley and tarragon
crusty bread, to serve

Takes 1¼–1½ hours • Serves 8

1 Heat the oil and butter in a large sauté pan and cook the chicken in batches for 3–4 minutes until golden all over. Remove from the pan and set aside. Add the shallots, garlic, potatoes and carrots to the pan and toss together. Cook for about 5 minutes until beginning to turn golden. Sprinkle over the flour, stir in the mustard and toss well, then pour over the white wine and gently simmer until reduced by about half.
2 Pour in the stock, bring to a simmer, then return the chicken to the pan. Cover and simmer for about 15 minutes.
3 Scatter over the asparagus and broad beans, without stirring, cover and simmer for a further 8 minutes. Stir in the lemon juice, cream, parsley and tarragon and heat through gently. Serve with crusty bread.

• Per serving 414 kcalories, protein 42g, carbohydrate 23g, fat 14g, saturated fat 6g, fibre 5g, added sugar none, salt 0.92g

Good-quality canned tomatoes really make a difference
to the flavour of this dish.

Spicy Lamb with Chickpeas

1.25kg/2lb 8oz boneless lamb fillet
or leg, cubed
2 × 400g cans tomatoes in rich juice
1 tbsp harissa paste, or to taste
2 × 410g cans chickpeas, drained
and rinsed
large handful of coriander, roughly
chopped

Takes 1½–1¾ hours • Serves 8

1 Put the lamb and tomatoes in a large pan.
Fill one of the tomato cans with water, pour
into the pan and stir in the harissa with a
good sprinkling of salt and pepper. Bring to
the boil, then reduce the heat and cover the
pan. Simmer gently, stirring occasionally, for
1¼–1½ hours or until the lamb is tender.
2 Tip in the chickpeas, stir well and heat
through for 5 minutes. Taste for seasoning,
adding more harissa if you like. Serve
scattered with coriander.

• Per serving 406 kcalories, protein 36g, carbohydrate
13g, fat 24g, saturated fat 10.8g, fibre 3.5g, added
sugar none, salt 0.82g

This is a quick variation of the classic Greek dish. For an authentic Mediterranean meal, serve with toasted pitta bread.

Hob-to-table Moussaka

2 tbsp olive oil
2 large onions, finely chopped
2 garlic cloves, finely chopped
1kg/2lb 4oz minced lamb
2 × 400g cans chopped tomatoes
3 tbsp tomato purée
2 tsp ground cinnamon
200g jar chargrilled aubergines in olive oil, drained and chopped
300g/10oz feta, crumbled
large handful of mint, chopped
green salad and toasted pitta bread, to serve

Takes 40–50 minutes • Serves 8

1 Heat the oil in a large deep frying pan or sauté pan. Toss in the onions and garlic and fry until soft. Add the mince and stir fry for about 10 minutes until browned.
2 Tip the tomatoes into the pan, add a canful of water and stir in the tomato purée and cinnamon. Season generously with salt and pepper. Leave the mince to simmer for 30 minutes, adding the aubergines halfway through.
3 Sprinkle the crumbled feta and chopped mint over the mince. Bring the moussaka to the table as the feta melts, and serve with a crunchy green salad and toasted pitta.

• Per serving 454 kcalories, protein 32g, carbohydrate 10g, fat 32g, saturated fat 14.1g, fibre 2.3g, added sugar none, salt 1.83g

Thai curries cook in just a few minutes once all the ingredients are prepared, so this is a one-pot dish you'll be cooking again and again.

Thai Green Chicken Curry

2 tbsp vegetable oil
2 garlic cloves, chopped
6 tsp Thai green curry paste
2 × 400ml cans coconut milk
450g/1lb new potatoes, scrubbed and cut into chunks
200g pack trimmed green beans, halved
4 tsp Thai fish sauce (*nam pla*), or to taste
2 tsp caster sugar
6 boneless, skinless chicken breasts, cut into large bite-sized pieces
2 fresh kaffir lime leaves, finely shredded, or 3 wide strips of lime zest
large handful of basil leaves

Takes 30–40 minutes • Serves 8

1 Heat the oil in a large wok, drop in the garlic and stir until just golden. Add the curry paste and stir for a couple of minutes, then pour in the coconut milk and bring to the boil. Add the potatoes and simmer for 10 minutes, then add the beans and simmer for 5 minutes more. Both the potatoes and beans should be just tender by now – if not, cook a little longer.
2 Stir in the fish sauce and sugar, then add the chicken, cover and simmer for 10 minutes until tender. Before serving, stir in the lime leaves or zest, followed by the basil. Taste and add more fish sauce if you like.

• Per serving 363 kcalories, protein 29g, carbohydrate 15g, fat 21g, saturated fat 14.6g, fibre 1.3g, added sugar 1.4g, salt 1.09g

Jars of artichokes in oil are a great storecupboard standby.
They work beautifully with the mint and tomato in this lamb medley.

Saucy Summer Lamb

1kg/2lb 4oz ripe tomatoes
1.25kg/2lb 4oz cubed lamb
(boneless neck, shoulder or leg)
3 tbsp olive oil
1 large Spanish onion, thinly sliced
290g jar artichoke hearts in oil, drained
large handful of mint leaves, roughly chopped

Takes 1¼–1½ hours • Serves 8

1 Make a cross in the bottom of each tomato with a sharp knife, then put a third of the tomatoes in a large bowl and cover with boiling water. Leave for a few minutes until the skins split, then drain and peel. Repeat with the remaining tomatoes, then chop them roughly.
2 Season the lamb. Heat 2 tablespoons of the oil in a large saucepan over a medium-high heat and fry the lamb in batches until browned. Put to one side. Lower the heat, add the remaining oil and the onion to the pan and fry for about 5 minutes until softened.
3 Return the lamb to the pan and stir in the tomatoes. Bring to the boil, lower the heat and splash in some hot water to cover the meat. Put the lid on and simmer for 50–60 minutes or until the lamb is tender. Stir in the artichokes and mint, heat through and season to taste.

• Per serving 405 kcalories, protein 31g, carbohydrate 7g, fat 28g, saturated fat 10.7g, fibre 2.3g, added sugar none, salt 0.68g

This is the magic formula for making cheaper cuts of meat meltingly tender.

Pork with Celeriac and Orange

1kg/2lb 4oz boneless pork shoulder, cut into bite-sized chunks

3 tbsp olive oil

1 large celeriac (about 1kg/2lb 4oz), peeled and chopped into large chunks

4 leeks, trimmed and chopped into chunks

3 carrots, peeled and chopped into chunks

2 garlic cloves, chopped

400ml/14fl oz dry white wine

400ml/14fl oz chicken stock

2 tbsp soy sauce

finely grated zest and juice of 1 large orange

large rosemary sprig

Takes 2½–2¾ hours • Serves 8

1 Preheat the oven to 140°C/Gas 1/fan oven 120°C. Season the meat well. Heat 1 tablespoon of the oil in a large flameproof casserole over a medium-high heat. Add half the pork and leave for a couple of minutes until browned underneath, then brown the other side for 2–3 minutes. Using a slotted spoon, transfer the pork to a plate. Repeat with another spoonful of oil and the remaining meat.
2 Heat the remaining oil in the pan and fry the vegetables and garlic for 3–4 minutes until starting to brown. Tip the pork and its juices into the pan, then add the remaining ingredients. Stir well and bring to the boil.
3 Cover the pan and cook in the oven for 2–2¼ hours until the pork is very tender, stirring halfway. Leave to stand for 10 minutes, taste for seasoning and serve.

• Per serving 251 kcalories, protein 29g, carbohydrate 11g, fat 10g, saturated fat 2.3g, fibre 6.9g, added sugar 0.1g, salt 1.39g

This dish tastes rather special for something that's so easy to make. As an alternative to goat's cheese you can use Boursin.

Chicken with Goat's Cheese

8 large skinless chicken breasts
20g pack fresh tarragon
2 × 150g cartons soft goat's cheese, such as Charvoux
5 vine-ripened tomatoes, sliced
3 tbsp olive oil
dressed salad leaves and bread, to serve

Takes 40–50 minutes • Serves 8

1 Preheat the oven to 200°C/Gas 6/fan oven 180°C. Make a slit down the centre of each chicken breast (taking care not to cut right through), then make a pocket with your fingers. Arrange the chicken in a single layer in a large, lightly oiled ovenproof dish.

2 Reserve 8 sprigs of tarragon, chop the rest of the leaves and beat into the cheese with plenty of black pepper. Spoon into the pockets in the chicken. Place 2 tomato slices over each cheese-filled pocket, put a tarragon sprig on top and drizzle with oil.

3 Season and bake for 25–30 minutes until the chicken is cooked, but still moist. Serve hot or cold with dressed salad leaves and bread.

• Per serving 248 kcalories, protein 34g, carbohydrate 2g, fat 12g, saturated fat 4g, fibre 1g, added sugar none, salt 0.64g

This is a brilliant way of stretching
a couple of packets of mince.

Beef and Bean Hotpot

750g/1lb 10oz lean minced beef
1 beef stock cube
2 large onions, roughly chopped
450g/1lb carrots, peeled and thickly sliced
1.25kg/2lb 8oz potatoes, peeled and cut into large chunks
2 × 400g cans baked beans
Worcestershire sauce or Tabasco, to taste
large handful of parsley, roughly chopped

Takes about 1 hour • Serves 8

1 Heat a large non-stick pan, add the beef and fry over a medium-high heat until browned, stirring often and breaking up any lumps with a spoon. Crumble in the stock cube and mix well.

2 Add the vegetables, stir to mix with the beef and pour in enough boiling water (about 1.2 litres/2 pints) to cover. Bring to the boil, then lower the heat and stir well. Cover the pan and simmer gently for about 30 minutes or until the vegetables are tender.

3 Tip in the baked beans, sprinkle with Worcestershire sauce or Tabasco to taste, stir well and heat through. Taste for seasoning and sprinkle with the parsley. Serve with extra Worcestershire sauce or Tabasco, for those who like a peppery hot taste.

• Per serving 362 kcalories, protein 31g, carbohydrate 51g, fat 5g, saturated fat 1.9g, fibre 7.9g, added sugar 3.4g, salt 2.05g

This soup is a meal in itself and it's sure to be a hit with its delicious aromas and wonderful flavours.

Moroccan Lamb Harira

100g/4oz dried chickpeas, soaked overnight and drained
100g/4oz Puy lentils
750g/1lb 10oz ready-diced lamb, cut into 1cm/½in cubes
1 large Spanish onion, finely chopped
1 tsp turmeric
½ tsp ground cinnamon
¼ tsp each ground ginger, saffron strands and paprika
50g/2oz butter
100g/4oz long-grain rice
4 large ripe tomatoes, peeled, seeded and chopped
2 tbsp chopped fresh coriander
4 tbsp chopped fresh flatleaf parsley
lemon quarters, to serve

Takes 2½–2¾ hours • Serves 8

1 Tip the chickpeas and lentils into a large saucepan or flameproof casserole. Add the lamb, onion and spices and pour in about 1.5 litres/2½ pints water – enough to cover the meat and pulses. Season.

2 Bring to the boil, skimming the froth from the surface as the water begins to bubble, then stir in half the butter. Turn down the heat and simmer, covered, for 2 hours until the chickpeas are tender, adding the rice and tomatoes for the last 30 minutes, with more water if necessary.

3 To finish, stir in the remaining butter with the coriander and parsley (hold a little back for a garnish if you like) and taste for seasoning. Serve hot, with a lemon quarter for each serving so guests can squeeze over lemon juice to taste.

• Per serving 370 kcalories, protein 25g, carbohydrate 28g, fat 18g, saturated fat 9.2g, fibre 3.6g, added sugar none, salt 0.27g

A great chilli has to be one of the best dishes to serve to friends for a casual get-together, and this one is even better made in advance.

Chilli con Carne

2 tbsp vegetable oil
1 large Spanish onion, finely chopped
2 red peppers, seeded and cut into 1cm/½in dice
2 garlic cloves, crushed
1–2 tsp chilli powder, to taste
2 tsp paprika
2 tsp ground cumin
1 tsp dried marjoram
900g/2lb minced beef
1 beef stock cube
2 × 400g cans chopped tomatoes
3 tbsp tomato purée
1 tsp sugar
2 × 410g cans red kidney beans, drained and rinsed

Takes about 1¼ hours • Serves 8

1 Heat the oil in a large, deep pan and gently fry the onion until softened. Add the red peppers, garlic, spices and marjoram and fry, stirring, for 5 minutes. Tip in the meat and increase the heat to high. Fry until all of the meat is browned, stirring often and breaking up any lumps with a spoon.
2 Crumble in the stock cube and pour in 600ml/1 pint water, then tip in the tomatoes and add the tomato purée and sugar. Stir well and bring to the boil. Cover and simmer for 30 minutes, stirring in a splash or two of hot water from the kettle if the meat becomes dry.
3 Stir in the beans and heat through, uncovered, for 10 minutes. Remove from the heat and taste for seasoning, then cover the pan. Leave to stand for 10–15 minutes before serving.

• Per serving 402 kcalories, protein 30g, carbohydrate 22g, fat 22g, saturated fat 8.5g, fibre 6.3g, added sugar 0.7g, salt 1.61g

A comforting and hearty dish that's perfect
for winter dinner parties.

Beef Paprikash

3 tbsp sunflower oil
1.5kg/3lb braising steak or stewing
beef, cut into 5cm/2in cubes
2 large onions, sliced
2 garlic cloves, crushed
2 rounded tbsp paprika
3 tbsp tomato purée
2 tbsp wine vinegar (red or white)
2 tsp dried marjoram or mixed herbs
2 bay leaves
½ tsp caraway seeds
2 × 400g cans chopped tomatoes or
2 × 500g jars passata
750ml/1¼ pints beef stock
2 large red peppers, seeded and cut
into rings
142ml carton soured cream

Takes 3–3½ hours • Serves 8

1 Preheat the oven to 160°C/Gas 3/fan oven
140°C. Heat 2 tablespoons of the oil in a
large flameproof casserole until very hot.
Brown the meat in 2–3 batches, removing
each batch with a slotted spoon.
2 Add the remaining oil, the onions and
garlic. Cook on a low heat for 10 minutes,
stirring now and then, until the onions soften.
Add the meat and juices and blend in the
paprika, tomato purée, vinegar, herbs, bay
leaves and caraway seeds.
3 Tip in the tomatoes, add the stock, season
and bring to the boil, adding some water if the
meat is not covered. Stir, cover, and put in the
oven for 2½ hours, or until the meat is tender.
Halfway through, stir in the red peppers. Serve
with dollops of soured cream.

• Per serving 451 kcalories, protein 43g, carbohydrate
14g, fat 25g, saturated fat 9.7g, fibre 2.8g, added
sugar none, salt 0.87g

Impress your friends with this sensational curry, which delivers a full rich flavour and authentic spiciness without the usual high-fat content.

Fragrant Chicken Curry

3 onions, quartered
4 fat garlic cloves
5cm/2in piece fresh root ginger, peeled and roughly chopped
3 tbsp moglai (medium) curry powder
1 tsp turmeric
2 tsp paprika
2 fresh red chillies, seeded and roughly chopped
2 × 20g packs fresh coriander
1 chicken stock cube
6 large boneless, skinless chicken breasts, cubed
2 × 410g cans chickpeas, drained and rinsed
natural low-fat yogurt, naan bread or poppadums, to serve

Takes 60–70 minutes • Serves 8

1 Tip the onions, garlic, ginger, curry powder, ground spices, chillies and half the coriander into a food processor. Add 1 teaspoon salt and blend to a purée (you may need to do this in 2 batches). Tip the mixture into a large saucepan and cook over a low heat for 10 minutes, stirring frequently.
2 Crumble in the stock cube, pour in 750ml/1¼ pints boiling water and return to the boil. Add the chicken, stir, then lower the heat and simmer for 20 minutes or until the chicken is tender.
3 Chop the remaining coriander, then stir all but about 2 tablespoons into the curry with the chickpeas. Heat through. Serve topped with the reserved coriander and the natural yogurt, with naan bread or poppadums on the side.

• Per serving 227 kcalories, protein 32g, carbohydrate 17g, fat 4g, saturated fat 0.4g, fibre 4.6g, added sugar none, salt 1.72g

Tender neck fillets of lamb are more expensive than pre-diced casserole lamb but do cut down on cooking time.

Lamb and Red Pepper Stew

1.25kg/2lb 8oz boneless lamb fillet, cut into small chunks
40g/1½oz plain flour, seasoned
3 tbsp olive oil
3 garlic cloves, crushed
300ml/½ pint dry white wine
3 large red peppers, seeded and cut into 5cm/2in pieces
500g jar passata (sieved tomatoes)
300ml/½ pint stock (lamb, chicken or vegetable)
3 bay leaves
175g/6oz ready-to-eat dried prunes or apricots

Takes 50–60 minutes • Serves 8

1 Coat the lamb in the seasoned flour, shaking off the excess. Heat 2 tablespoons of the oil in a large saucepan until hot. Tip in a third of the lamb and fry over a medium-high heat, turning occasionally, until browned. Transfer to a plate with a slotted spoon and repeat with the remaining lamb, adding the remaining oil when necessary.
2 Return all the meat to the pan, sprinkle in the garlic and cook for 1 minute. Pour in the wine and, scraping up any residue, cook over a high heat until reduced by about a third. Stir in the remaining ingredients except the dried fruit. Cover and simmer for 30–40 minutes or until the lamb is tender.
3 Stir in the dried fruit and heat through for 5 minutes, then taste for seasoning before serving.

• Per serving 497 kcalories, protein 31g, carbohydrate 22g, fat 32g, saturated fat 14.5g, fibre 2.7g, added sugar 0.9g, salt 0.69g

Marinating the strawberries in the Beaujolais gives them a lovely flavour, but don't do it too far ahead or they will lose their texture.

Beaujolais Berries

700g/1lb 9oz strawberries, hulled and halved
3 tbsp golden caster sugar
handful of mint leaves, plus a few extra
½ bottle Beaujolais

Takes 5–10 minutes, plus marinating • Serves 6

1 Lay the strawberries in a bowl and sprinkle over the caster sugar. Scatter over a handful of mint leaves and let the strawberries sit for about 30 minutes so they start to release their juices.

2 Pour the Beaujolais over the strawberries and scatter over a few more fresh mint leaves. Leave for another 10 minutes before serving.

• Per serving 102 kcalories, protein 1g, carbohydrate 15g, fat 1g, saturated fat none, fibre 1g, added sugar 8g, salt 0.03g

To make this tasty pudding extra fruity, slice up a couple of pears or a cooking apple (with a sprinkling of sugar) and stir into the fruit.

Cookie-dough Crumble

500g bag mixed frozen fruit
350g pot fresh cookie dough (chocolate chip is good)
cream, ice cream or custard, to serve

Takes 20–25 minutes • Serves 4

1 Preheat the oven to 220°C/Gas 7/fan oven 200°C. Tip the frozen fruit into a shallow baking dish and tear pieces of dough all over the top.
2 Bake for 20 minutes until crisp and golden. Serve with cream, ice cream or custard.

• Per serving 457 kcalories, protein 8g, carbohydrate 57g, fat 24g, saturated fat 13g, fibre 6g, added sugar 9g, salt 1.2g

To make small puddings, simply tear the bread roughly and layer up with the fruit in individual ramekins. Turn out or serve as they are.

Simple Summer Pudding

450g/1lb summer berries, defrosted if frozen
4 tbsp blackcurrant cordial or crème de cassis
225g carton chilled red fruits compote
6 medium slices white bread, crusts cut off

Takes 40–50 minutes • Serves 4

1 Mix the berries, cordial and compote and leave for 5–10 minutes. If you are using defrosted fruit, mix in some of the juice.
2 Line a 1.2 litre/2 pint pudding bowl with cling film, letting it hang over the sides. Cut a circle from one of the slices of bread to fit the base of the bowl, then cut the remaining slices into quarters.
3 Drain the juice from the fruit into a bowl and dip the bread into it until soaked. Layer the fruit and bread in the bowl and pour over the remaining juice. Cover with the overhanging cling film. Put a small plate or saucer on top to fit inside the rim of the bowl, then stand a couple of heavy cans on top to press it down. Chill in the refrigerator for at least 10 minutes, or until you are ready to eat (it will keep for up to 24 hours).

• Per serving 201 kcalories, protein 5g, carbohydrate 46g, fat 1g, saturated fat 0.2g, fibre 5g, added sugar 11g, salt 0.6g

Everyone will fall in love with this recipe! It's hard to believe that something that tastes this good can take so little time and effort to make.

Tiramisu Trifle

300ml/½ pint strong, good-quality black coffee
175ml/6fl oz Disaronno (amaretto) liqueur
500g carton mascarpone
500g/1lb 2oz good-quality fresh custard
250g/9oz Savoiardi biscuits (Italian sponge fingers) or sponge fingers
85g/3oz good-quality dark chocolate, roughly chopped

TO DECORATE
4 tbsp toasted slivered almonds
chopped dark chocolate

Takes 10–15 minutes, plus chilling • Serves 8–10

1 Mix the coffee and liqueur in a wide dish. Beat the mascarpone and custard together in a bowl with a hand blender or whisk.
2 Take a third of the biscuits and dip each one into the coffee mix until soft but not soggy. Line the bottom of a glass trifle dish with the biscuits and drizzle over more of the coffee mixture.
3 Sprinkle a third of the chocolate over the biscuits, then follow with a layer of the mascarpone mixture. Repeat twice more. Chill in the fridge for at least 2 hours (preferably overnight). Sprinkle with the almonds and chocolate before serving.

• Per serving for eight 624 kcalories, protein 8g, carbohydrate 54g, fat 39g, saturated fat 23g, fibre 1g, added sugar 35g, salt 0.38g

Choose firm plums for this recipe – if they are overripe they will ooze too much juice and you will have a flood on your kitchen worktop.

Plum and Marzipan Tarte Tatin

25g/1oz butter
25g/1oz golden caster sugar
800g/1lb 12oz firm plums, not too ripe, halved and stoned
100g/4oz golden marzipan
40g/1½oz ground almonds
500g pack puff pastry, thawed if frozen
pouring cream (single or double), to serve

Takes about 1–1¼ hours • Serves 6–8

1 Preheat the oven to 200°C/Gas 6/fan oven 180°C. Melt the butter in a 28cm/11in tarte tatin tin over a medium heat. Tip in the sugar and 1 tablespoon water and stir for a few minutes until lightly browned. Remove from the heat and put in the plums, cut side up.
2 Chop the marzipan into as many chunks as there are plum halves, put a chunk into each plum and sprinkle over the ground almonds.
3 Roll out the pastry and trim to 4cm/1½in larger than the tin all round. Lift the pastry onto the tin and tuck it down between the plums and the inside of the tin. Bake for 30–35 minutes until the pastry is risen, crisp and golden. Cool for 10 minutes, then place a large flat plate with a rim over the tin. Holding it over the sink in case of drips, invert the tarte onto the plate. Serve with cream.

• Per serving for six 511 kcalories, protein 8g, carbohydrate 58g, fat 29g, saturated fat 3g, fibre 3g, added sugar 13g, salt 0.75g

The lovely colours and fabulous flavours of this one-pot pudding will really surprise you.

Tropical Fruit Salad

1 ripe papaya
1 small pineapple
12 cape gooseberries (physalis)
50g/2oz butter
4 tbsp light or dark muscovado sugar
4 tbsp coconut rum (or white or dark rum) or pineapple and coconut juice
seeds of 1 pomegranate
vanilla or rum and raisin ice cream, to serve

Takes 25–30 minutes •
Serves 4

1 Halve the papaya lengthways and scoop out the seeds, then peel the fruit and cut into slim wedges. Cut off the top, bottom and skin of the pineapple, and remove all the eyes from the flesh. Cut the pineapple lengthways into wedges and slice the core off the edge of each wedge. Cut each wedge crossways into chunks. Remove the papery husks from the cape gooseberries.
2 Melt the butter and sugar in a wide deep pan, add the prepared fruit and toss until coated and glistening. Sprinkle over the rum or fruit juice and the pomegranate seeds, and shake the pan to distribute evenly. Serve hot, with ice cream.

• Per serving 308 kcalories, protein 2g, carbohydrate 45g, fat 11g, saturated fat 6.5g, fibre 4.8g, added sugar 15.2g, salt 0.22g

Serve the clafoutis barely warm to get the best
from the subtle flavours.

Cherry Vanilla Clafoutis

650g/1lb 7oz fresh cherries (dark,
juicy ones)
4 tbsp golden caster sugar
4 tbsp kirsch
3 large eggs
50g/2oz plain flour
150ml/¼ pint milk
200ml carton crème fraîche (full or
half fat)
1 tsp vanilla extract
icing sugar, for dusting

Takes 1–1¼ hours • Serves 6

1 Preheat the oven to 190°C/Gas 5/fan oven
170°C. Stone the cherries, but try to keep
them whole.
2 Scatter the cherries over the base of a
buttered shallow ovenproof dish, about 1 litre/
1¾ pints capacity. Sprinkle the cherries with
1 tablespoon each of sugar and kirsh.
3 Whisk the eggs with an electric beater or
hand whisk until they are soft and foamy –
about 1–2 minutes. Whisk in the flour and
remaining sugar, then add the remaining
kirsch, the milk, crème fraîche and vanilla
extract.
4 Pour the batter over the cherries and bake
for 35–40 minutes until pale golden. Leave to
cool to room temperature, then dust lightly
with icing sugar and serve just warm.

• Per serving 309 kcalories, protein 7g, carbohydrate
35g, fat 14g, saturated fat 7g, fibre 1g, added sugar
15g, salt 0.23g

Splash a few tablespoons of armagnac or brandy over the figs before grilling to make a boozy pudding.

Sticky Cinnamon Figs

8 ripe figs
large knob of butter
4 tbsp clear honey
handful shelled pistachio nuts or almonds
1 tsp ground cinnamon or mixed spice
mascarpone or Greek yogurt, to serve

Takes 10 minutes • Serves 4

1 Preheat the grill to medium high. Cut a deep cross in the top of each fig, then ease the top apart like a flower. Sit the figs in a baking dish and drop a small piece of the butter into the centre of each fruit. Drizzle the honey over the figs, then sprinkle with the nuts and spice.

2 Grill for 5 minutes until the figs are softened and the honey and butter make a sticky sauce in the bottom of the dish. Serve warm, with dollops of mascarpone or yogurt.

• Per serving 162 kcalories, protein 3g, carbohydrate 23g, fat 7g, saturated fat 2g, fibre 2g, added sugar 11.5g, salt 0.06g

This recipe has all the elements of a summer pudding, but is much simpler, and served hot. The jammy smells as it cooks are wonderful.

Grilled Summer Berry Pudding

4 slices white sliced bread, crusts removed
85g/3oz golden caster sugar
2 tsp cornflour
200g carton low-fat fromage frais
300g/10oz mixed summer berries (such as raspberries, blueberries, redcurrants, sliced strawberries) or 300g/10oz frozen berries, defrosted

Takes 20–30 minutes • Serves 4

1 Preheat the grill to high. Lay the slices of bread slightly overlapping in a shallow flameproof dish. Sprinkle about 2 tablespoons of the sugar over the bread and grill for about 2 minutes until the bread is toasted and the sugar is starting to caramelise. Mix the cornflour into the fromage frais.
2 Pile the fruit down the middle of the bread and sprinkle with 1 tablespoon of the sugar. Drop spoonfuls of the fromage frais mixture on top, then sprinkle over the rest of the sugar.
3 Put the dish as close to the heat as you can and grill for 6–8 minutes until the fromage frais has browned and everything else is starting to bubble and turn juicy. Leave for a minute or two before serving.

• Per serving 211 kcalories, protein 7g, carbohydrate 47g, fat 1g, saturated fat none, fibre 2g, added sugar 22g, salt 0.45g

This special treat of a dessert makes a good alternative to Christmas pudding. Serve it with crème fraîche or vanilla ice cream.

Spicy Steamed Fruit Pudding

1 cup raisins
1 cup sultanas
1 cup self-raising flour
1 cup finely grated cold butter
(about 100g/4oz), plus extra at
room temperature for greasing
1 cup fresh brown breadcrumbs
(from around 4 thick slices bread)
1 cup light muscovado sugar
1 cup mixed nuts, chopped
(optional)
1 tsp ground cinnamon
1 tsp ground mixed spice
1 cup milk
1 large egg

TO SERVE (OPTIONAL)
butterscotch or caramel sauce
handful of mixed nuts

Takes 2½–3 hours • Serves 8–10

1 Using a 300ml/½ pint coffee mug as your cup measure, empty the first 6 cups and the nuts, if using, into a bowl with the spices, then stir in the milk and egg until well combined. Tip into a buttered 1.5 litre/2¾ pint pudding bowl.
2 Cover with a double layer of buttered foil, making a pleat in the centre to allow the pudding to rise. Tie with string, then place in a steamer or large pan with enough gently simmering water to come halfway up the sides of the bowl. Cover and steam for 2½ hours, adding more water as necessary.
3 To serve, unwrap the pudding and invert onto a deep plate, then drizzle with sauce and decorate the top with nuts, if using.

• Per serving for eight 423 kcalories, protein 6g, carbohydrate 75g, fat 13g, saturated fat 7.9g, fibre 1.8g, added sugar 28.5g, salt 0.66g

Index

Picture credits and recipe credits

BBC Worldwide would like to thank the following for providing photographs. While every effort has been made to trace and acknowledge all photographers, we would like to apologize should there be any errors or omissions.

Marie-Louise Avery p23, p51, p133; Iain Bagwell p27, p97, p107; Steve Baxter p13, p53, p113, p159; Martin Brigdale p183; Carl Clemens-Gros p105, p177; Ken Field p11, p15, p43, p47, p55, p67, p101, p117, p123, p135, p141, p171; Will Heap p89, p207; Dave King p131; William Lingwood p29, p119; Jason Lowe p37, p197; David Munns p25, p35, p49, p61, p69, p111, p167, p179, p209; Myles New p143; Myles New & Craig Robertson p19; Craig Robertson p185, p199, p203; Howard Shooter p91; Sharon Smith p137; Roger Stowell p21, p31, p39, p45, p65, p73, p75, p77, p83, p85, p93, p99, p109, p115, p121, p127, p151, p153, p155, p163, p181, p191, p205, p211; Sam Stowell p187; Simon Walton p41, p59, p173; Cameron Watt p157; Philip Webb p17, p33, p57, p71, p79, p81, p89, p95, p103, p129, p145, p147, p149, p165, p195; Simon Wheeler p63, p139, p161, p169, p175, p189, p193, p201; Jonathan Whittaker p87.

All the recipes in this book have been created by the editorial team on *BBC Good Food Magazine*:

Lorna Brash, Sara Buenfeld, Mary Cadogan, Barney Desmazery, Jane Hornby, Emma Lewis, Kate Moseley, Orlando Murrin, Vicky Musselman, Angela Nilsen, Maggie Pannell, Jenny White, Jeni Wright.